THE HEALING

POWER OF JOY

ALSO BY RON SCOLASTICO, PH.D.

YOUR SPIRITUAL TEMPLE
Being A Soul In A Physical Body

COSMIC MOMENTS
Inspiring Reminders of Your Eternal Nature

BECOMING ENLIGHTENED
Twelve Keys to Higher Consciousness

THE MYSTERY OF THE CHRIST FORCE
A Personal Story of Enlightenment
for Spiritual Seekers

DOORWAY TO THE SOUL
How to Have a Profound Spiritual Experience

REFLECTIONS
Inspired Wisdom on: Gods and Symbols;
The Human Mind; Angels and Guides;
Education; Healing Addictions;
and, Healing the Hurt Child

HEALING THE HEART,
HEALING THE BODY
A Spiritual Perspective on Emotional,
Mental, and Physical Health

THE EARTH ADVENTURE
Your Soul's Journey Through Physical Reality

The Wisdom of the Guides

The Retreat Series: Volume 2

THE HEALING POWER OF JOY

A Spiritual Perspective

Ron Scolastico, Ph.D.

UNIVERSAL GUIDANCE PRESS

The Wisdom of the Guides
The Retreat Series: Volume 2

THE HEALING POWER OF JOY
A Spiritual Perspective

UNIVERSAL GUIDANCE PRESS
P.O. Box 6556
Woodland Hills, California 91365
www.ronscolastico.com
1-818-224-4488

Library of Congress Cataloging-in-Publication Data
Scolastico, Ronald B. (Ronald Barry)
The Healing Power Of Joy/
Ron Scolastico

1. Spiritual life. 2. Experience (Religion) 3. Self-realization—
Religious aspects. I. Title.

ISBN 978-0-943833-27-9

Joy, rather than happiness, is the goal of life,
for joy is the emotion which accompanies
our fulfilling our natures as human beings.
It is based on the experience of one's identity
as a being of worth and dignity.

Dr. Rollo May

For Susan

CONTENTS

PREFACE

DR. RON SCOLASTICO is a distinguished spiritual psychologist, philosopher, and author who has studied human consciousness for more than forty years. After conducting extensive research into the theoretical aspects of transpersonal psychology, and through a number of years of personal experience with altered states of consciousness, in 1978 he learned to enter a deep state of expanded consciousness to draw upon a vast source of transpersonal wisdom to provide spiritual and psychological guidance for individuals and groups. In describing his personal experience with this spiritual counseling, Dr. Scolastico says:

> "In the work that I have done in the transpersonal dimension for more than thirty years, I have experienced the spiritual realm as an extraordinary non-physical reality that manifests to my consciousness as a magnificent, perfect, all-pervasive 'environment,' or 'force.' In more than twenty-thousand engagements with this *Causative Force*, I have consistently experienced the grandeur of this reality as what I can only describe in any tangible way as the most beautiful 'radiance,' but a radiance that is permeated with *perfect love*, and with a seemingly unending source of cosmic wisdom. From these many

experiences, I have become convinced of what people in all cultures throughout the ages have believed: *The Causative Force of life is an extraordinarily loving spiritual force that exists in a non-physical dimension,* and, *human beings are an extension of that force.*"

When Dr. Scolastico does his spiritual counseling from the deep state of consciousness, he calls the session a "Reading" in order to distinguish it from counseling done in the fully conscious state. When he does a Reading, he says, "I experience myself floating into the extraordinary transpersonal dimension from which words of wisdom are spoken that go far beyond my ordinary knowledge and personal experience."

For the sake of simplicity, he thinks of the source of the wisdom that he taps in to as spiritual guides. Thus, the body of knowledge from the Readings is called, "The Wisdom of the Guides."

The books in the **"Wisdom of the Guides Retreat Series"** present a collection of knowledge taken from special group Readings given by Dr. Scolastico at the annual five-day "Spiritual Retreat With The Guides," conducted at the Serra Retreat Center in Malibu, California.

This second volume in the series, *The Healing Power of Joy,* presents the transcripts of ten Readings done by Dr. Scolastico at the 17th. Annual Retreat in November, 2001. In this Retreat, the readings explored in great depth the profound mystery of joy as a spiritual practice in daily life. Some of the intriguing and important topics addressed in these Readings include:

Your Personal Power to Create Joy,
Celebrating the Intensity of Your Human Experience,
Acceptance of Human Negative Experience,
Creating the Experience of Fun,
Joy and Your Physical Health,
Awakening Cellular Consciousness in the Body,
Transforming Divine Energy Into Physical Matter,
Awakening to Eternal Timelessness,
Learning the True Purpose of Human Life on Earth,
Becoming Your Own Spiritual Teacher,
Creating an Ongoing Dialogue With Your Soul,
Four Keys to Greater Joy,
An Attunement to Divine Joy,
and much more.

DR. RON SCOLASTICO is a graduate of the University of California at Berkeley, received M.A. and Ph.D. degrees from the University of Iowa, and has studied at the University of Bordeaux, France. He is the author of numerous books and hundreds of audio recordings on many subjects. The wisdom of the Guides has been spoken through Dr. Scolastico in thousands of spiritual Readings given for individuals and groups around the world.

CHAPTER 1

The First Reading

NOTE: The ten Readings presented in this volume of "The Retreat Series" were done by Dr. Ron Scolastico over a five-day period. Most of these Readings consist of three parts: (1) the Guides' opening teaching; (2) questions asked by retreat participants, and the Guides' answers to those questions; and (3) a closing teaching by the Guides. In this first Reading, "The Guides' Beginning Teaching," no questions were asked. This transcript has been edited by Dr. Scolastico. In some cases, brief passages from other Readings were added to clarify a point.

The Guides' Beginning Teaching

As you ones focus upon the healing power of joy, you would be wise to first examine more thoroughly your present human *self.* Your experience of your *self* is often as though you have been given a large and very valuable golden coin. At first, you would rejoice in that coin, and you would feel quite wealthy. But, after you have carried that coin about for a long period of time, you grow very accustomed to it. There is a kind of *familiarity* about it, and the *value* of it seems to be less to you.

Since you have become so familiar with the coin of your personal *self* experience that you have carried about for a number of years in this lifetime, you do not realize that your *human-self-energy-structure* in your physical body is a most precious and extremely valuable gift that has been given to you by your soul. It is *you* as a unique individual. When you do not recognize the great value of yourself as that wonderful individual, then you squeeze the joy out of your life.

At times, you ones have appreciated the value of yourself as an important human being walking on earth, and that has expanded your experience of joy. At other times, you have taken yourself for granted. And, some of you have even been quite adept at consistently *condemning* yourself, effectively squeezing the joy out of your life.

As you ones come forth now to penetrate some of the deepest mysteries of the human experience, which have to do with awakening to Divine Perfection and its expression as human joy, if you could feel the reality of the extraordinary spiritual energies that constantly pour into you, then you would feel joyful in every moment. To understand why you do *not* feel that constant joy, there is the need to look at how much you have valued or devalued your coin of your human personality *self*.

In the beginning of this investigation together, if you notice that you have been *consistently* devaluing yourself for a while, then that becomes the most potent adjustment that you can make for stimulating more joy in your life. If you have been moderately devaluing yourself, or moderately *self-diminishing*, then a greater appreciation of yourself can bring moderate increases in joy. If you have been celebrating yourself rather consistently, then this focus would bring familiar levels of joy.

Yet, in this time together, no matter what your level of self-appreciation might be, we will show you a number of ways to awaken to your true magnificence as a human *self*, and this will begin to awaken you more fully to the extraordinary healing power of joy that you can bring into your life.

❖

All ones can begin their awakening with this reminder of the deeper *truth* of yourself by saying:

> **"I have come into this earth to express the Forces of God in a human *self* that manifests through my ability to think, to feel, to choose, to act, to do in life. My human experience was intended by my soul to be *a joyful celebration* of life on earth. As I begin to examine my own human *self* in its many complexities, I will now notice whether I have been celebrating joy enough in my life."**

If you have rather *consistently* celebrated your life in joy through the years, then you most likely are not diminishing yourself in dramatic ways. So, you will simply make a kind of promise in this moment to continue appreciating yourself, and to notice and adjust some of the smaller threads that can return in which you would say, "I am not good enough, I am not loveable, I am not fulfilling important purposes."

If you have been consistently celebrating your life, then any self-diminishment patterns that return will be mostly small. You would simply monitor your thoughts and feelings to adjust those patterns, and you would continue expanding your appreciation of yourself. As you do that, you can begin to stimulate your awareness of Divine Energies that sustain your subjective experience of you as a human *self.*

If you feel that you are not experiencing much of God Itself, that would be linked to not rejoicing enough in *you.* Most likely, you are self-diminishing.

If you notice that you are moderately self-diminishing, then you need to give a bit more attention to unleashing your capacity for greater joy upon the habits of criticizing yourself. You need to joyfully adjust your self-diminishing thoughts and feelings. This means that you first simply notice them. You pay *attention* to them to discover what they are.

Then, in moments of silence, you fully *experience* your self-diminishing thoughts and feelings for five or ten moments. You may wish to say them out loud to someone your trust. Then, you *release* those thoughts and feelings, and you say to yourself:

> **"These are not truths about the nature of my
> human *self.* They are my temporary thoughts
> and feelings that I have created in confusion**

**about who I am on this earth. I now release
these confusions, and I remember that** *I am a
wonderful human self who is a magnificent extension of my eternal soul."*

As you investigate your human *self*, your golden
coin, if you notice that you have been rather
consistently self-diminishing, then there needs to be
quite a bit of attention given to the conscious
celebration of you as a living human being. You need
to remind yourself quite often each day that the
golden coin of your human *self* is quite precious, quite
rare, quite valuable. Notice that you have been mostly
feeling that it is cheap, un-valuable, unimportant.
You have been feeling poor when you are truly
wealthy.

So, you need quite a bit of attention given to the
awakening to the *true majesty* of yourself. This is one
of the more difficult challenges for those human
beings who have consistently self-diminished and
who have not looked deeply into the true goodness of
their human *self.*

❖

Now, as you ones continue beyond your assessment
of your personal level of self-diminishment, or your
level of self-appreciation, the next stage in drawing
upon the healing power of joy is to recognize the
"fickleness" of the human personal *self* experience.
Let us say that it is as if the *self* is not only a golden
coin, but, it is one that has a mind of its own, and it
often hides itself away. So, when you wish to examine

it closely, it has hidden itself.

The mental-emotional makeup of you is not simply as a human that began in an infant birth as a "blank slate." Even in an infant who has just emerged from the womb and has been alive for only ten moments, there is an extraordinary complexity to the *personality-self-energy-structure* within that physical body. That complexity will continue to awaken and expand within that human being as the infant body grows.

So, you do not begin your human life as a clean slate. You begin as a complex tapestry of "energy," woven of so many different threads. And, *you-as-a-soul* have woven that tapestry.

Those human *self* energy threads are the many experiences, memories, tendencies, thought patterns, emotional patterns, likes, dislikes, fears—all of those different areas—that come from many *past* lifetimes that you have lived on earth. *You-as-a-soul* will orchestrate the most important of those countless threads, weaving them into your present human personality *self* energy structure that was inserted into your infant body after physical birth.

Thus, you can see that you come forth into your present human life immediately with a great complexity of many different inner patterns—innate talents, abilities, tendencies—that you will work with in this lifetime.

❖

Now, playfully speaking, as your infant body grows

through the years, in the *personal self experience* of you, there can come a kind of fickleness, particularly in your *desires*. This strongly influences your experience of joy.

First, you strongly desire some particular thing that you believe will bring you joy. Then, you achieve that desire fulfillment. For a while, as you achieve that, it is wonderful and you feel very joyful. Then, the joy fades away and you are not satisfied enough. So, you desire something else. You achieve that. You have some joy, then that feeling goes away. Then, you begin to desire something else. On and on this process goes throughout your human lifetime.

Your human *self* experience can also involve *fear*, which, of course, affects your experience of joy. You can be frightened of a certain thing, and you work diligently to eliminate that thing. When you eliminate that, you are no longer frightened. Then, you become frightened of something else. You work hard to eliminate that. When you succeed, you are no longer frightened until something else fearful comes along. So, working with fear will be necessary in order to draw the power of joy more fully into your life.

❖

Back and forth you ones go in the complexity of your human inner experience. Some try to *control* the fluctuations of human experience. They are the overly-watchful human ones who are usually the stubborn, stiffer ones who are less creative, less adventurous. Those who wish to *fully* engage life are usually the most changeable, or fickle, for they ride the rise and fall of the constantly changing tide of subjective experience.

As you work with yourself in bringing forth the healing power of joy, you must become more comfortable with the fluctuations of your inner experience of thoughts and feelings. You can gracefully accept the fact that one day you can be very happy, and then, after a while, you can be very sad, or even depressed. You understand that having strong negative feelings is not the end of life as you know it. You realize that you will not suddenly be destroyed if you have a dramatic change in your subjective experience in which joy has vanished and now you feel hopelessness and despair.

You can say to yourself, "If I am a passionate human living my life to the fullest, I can expect dramatic changes in my inner experience, given the complexity of the many different patterns within me." You need not fall into despair because you cannot constantly be joyful. You can actually appreciate the fact that you are so dramatic and fascinating in your strong subjective experiences. You can learn to have more relaxation with any dramatic changes in mood, in thought, in feeling, in responses to life.

Even when you are feeling miserable, you can actually be a bit more "joyful" about being miserable, for you can say, "The more intensely miserable I am now, the more it means that I am living my emotional life to the fullest. I am not squeezing my feelings. I am not running away from challenging negative feelings. I am experiencing them very strongly. This means that when my mood shifts, I will have very strong *positive* feelings."

❖

Achieving true joy in your life is not a matter of constantly striving to eliminate your negative thoughts and feelings so that you can always feel happy. It is more *a joyful celebration of the intensity of your human experience.*

Now, we would not expect that when you are in despair, deeply grieving, or terribly sad, that you would laugh, and sing, and feel wonderful. You will need to fully experience your negative feelings when you have them and live through them. But, as you are doing that, you could create the *thought*, "It is so satisfying to be an intense human, even when I feel miserable." That mental effort, in a sense, "glamorizes" your negativity and makes a certain sense of purpose to it. That also issues you a creative challenge of, "How can I be joyful when I am miserable?" There are endless possibilities for using your mind to not allow negative experience to squeeze the joy our of your life.

When you look at these areas, you could say, "I will not create more joy in my life by frantically trying to eliminate un-joyful experiences. I need to embrace them even more strongly, feel them more fully."

You might choose to spend less time creating

negative feelings, but, when they do arise, you need to feel them fully and completely so that you do not become afraid of having negative feelings. When you squeeze your feelings to avoid negative ones, you become emotionally tight and therefore cannot feel the joyful feelings as intensely.

True joy comes not, as many humans would believe, from the elimination of all that troubles you. It comes from the full and courageous embracing of *everything* that you experience—at least celebrating its *intensity* whether it pleases you or not.

If you prefer to work diligently to try to eliminate all negative experience from your life, then certainly you are free to make that choice. And, at times you might achieve it. But, at other times, you will not. So, if you would frantically say, "I *must* eliminate all negative experiences in order to have joy," then you will not have that much joy, for the dramatic, complex fluctuations of your human experience will often bring you experiences that are *not* joyful, things in your life that you cannot eliminate, particularly if you have challenges in your life in the outer physical world.

So, there is a certain kind of *patience* needed. There is needed a kind of gentle acceptance of your negative experience when it comes. It is as though you have made a child. And, you wish a most *beautiful* child. But, as the child grows, at times, it seems quite ugly. You do not say, "I will throw this child away because it is ugly," or, "I will kill this child." You *love* that child. You are not so happy that the child is ugly, but, you have the patience and the love for the child, and you rejoice in the child even if it is ugly."

In the same way, at times, you can seem ugly to yourself—in some of your thoughts, your feelings, your choices, your actions. In those times, you might say, "I am so terrible. I will not rejoice in me. I will beat myself, and punish myself until I become more beautiful."

Certainly, you can see that there is no benefit in that. Instead, you need to look closely at *your true inner goodness*, and you need to say, "At times, I can feel quite miserable, and that is part of my *intensity* as a human. It is part of my fascinating personality. So, I will be very patient and tolerant of the ugly child that I see in me when I pass through these kinds of moods."

❖

The next focus for creating more joy in your life is a certain sense of *freedom*. Mostly, you ones would experience freedom when you are not constrained by the necessities of your life in the physical world, or by the demands of other persons. But, if you would look closely, you would find that you actually have the ultimate freedom. You have the freedom to control your *inner* life, and, in a way, your physical body, and even your death.

You are free to cause suicide to your body at any time. You are free to make health or un-health by the care and feeding of your body. You are free to retreat from life. You are free to engage life. You are, most of you, free to go here and there physically. You are free to say this, or not say that. There is so much freedom that you have.

The deepest freedom, which is the large key to joy, is that you ones have the freedom to *think* anything that pleases you. Most of the time, you do not notice that freedom, for you are dominated by your *habits* of thought.

For example, imagine that you have the habit of thinking, "I am too heavy in the weight of my body, therefore, I am not lovable." At times, that thought can seem to take on a life of its own. It can dominate you. You can allow your mind to continually return to that thought, forgetting that you have the freedom to think anything that pleases you.

When you wish to create more joy in your life, it is not that you must eliminate negative thoughts and force joyful ones. You simply need to remember that you have the freedom to think anything that pleases you in any moment.

First, you must *notice* the habits of thinking that dominate you, then you can decide if you wish to change them. Imagine that you have a strong habit of thinking, "Human life on earth is quite meaningless. There is no purpose that I can see. I have been sad for many years. Nothing seems to bring me joy." If that is a thought pattern that you create each morning, then you need to understand that if you did *not* create those thoughts in the morning, you would not have the sense of meaninglessness. You could have different thoughts, and thereby a different experience. You are free to say, "Does it please me to think today that life is meaningless just because I have thought that for many years? Or, does it please me to have some new thoughts today?"

Most of you would, in this example, say, "The reason that I think life is meaningless is because I *feel* that life is meaningless." Observing this response opens the way to realizing that you also have the freedom to *feel* what pleases you.

Many of you ones feel that feelings are forced upon you by life. If a one is unkind to you, then you *must* feel terrible. If they are kind to you, then you must feel goodness. This is simply "training." You have been trained by your society, your family, about what to feel under certain circumstances. As a result of that training, most of you do not yet realize that you have the freedom to feel what you desire to feel.

You ones have the freedom to feel anything. To exercise that freedom, you need to look at what you believe causes you to feel something and then decide why that does occur that way. Then, you need to decide what you wish to do about the feelings, no matter what you believe caused them.

❖

If you would say, "I wish to feel more joy in my life," then you can begin to experiment with sitting in silence for a time each day to practice using your thoughts and emotions to actually *create* an experience of joy. You do not need to be perfectly satisfied with your life in the world to do this. You do not need to have a perfect fulfillment of all of your desires. You have the Forces of God Itself pouring into your human *self*, giving you the ability to think and feel. You are not a slave to your life circumstances, or to your mental and emotional habits.

You are an eternal being, temporarily expressing as your human *self* on earth. You personally wield the power of God, but, temporarily, you wield it within the "narrower" framework of being one human *self* creating your unique subjective experience moment by moment. As you create that all-important inner experience, understand that feelings need not be imposed upon you. They can be *chosen* by you. And, you can freely and consistently choose feelings of *joy*. You can practice *creating* feelings of joy as often as you like.

❖

Now, there are certain emotional responses in you ones that you might consider to be "automatic," or spontaneous, or instinctive. If a friend embraces you and says to you, "I love you," usually, that will stir feelings of joy within you. You do not consciously create those feelings. They are simply natural human responses.

So, in a sense, there are certain normal human responses that will create feelings for you. Depending upon the circumstances, some of those feelings can be joyful and some of them can be painful. Yet, you are also the master of such feelings after you have them. You can *choose* to allow those "natural" feelings to go forward and live them very simply and spontaneously without thinking about them at all. You can choose to allow those feelings to be whatever they naturally are. That is one way to live.

Or, you can consciously decide which of those kinds of feelings you will emphasize and promote, and which ones you will choose to release. In a most rare instance, you ones could lovingly and creatively choose *every* feeling that you have in this lifetime, and no feelings would be "imposed" upon you by other persons or by outer circumstances. That would be a bit beyond most ones on earth at this time, but, it is possible, and may be attained in the future.

❖

The next area to look at in your awakening to joy has to do with healing a sense of *isolation*. That sensation is an "artifact" of coming into a single human body, and playing out the role of *one* individual *self* who, temporarily, appears to be separate from all that is— particularly separate from other humans.

This is simply a condition that you ones have "agreed to" before coming into earth. Using your freedom, each of you must personally decide what you wish to do about that sense of isolation.

If you would choose to say, "It appears to me that all humans are separate and isolated, and it will *always* be so," then, that is what you will live. You will have the ongoing experience of being isolated. That is not a truth, but, that is what you will live because of the attitude that you take toward that innate sense of isolation.

On the other hand, you could say, "It *appears* that all humans are separate and isolated, and that does not please me. But, I can change my perceptions and discover ways in which I am joined to all ones."

Certainly, this is facilitated by warm, meaningful relationships with other humans. The closer and deeper those relationships are, the more you can begin to feel, "Perhaps there is no actual separation. Perhaps separation is an illusion."

If you could actually feel the *truth*, you would be joyful constantly, for you would know that as a *being*, you are woven with every being in every realm by extraordinary threads and fabrics of *Divine Love* that are never broken. You would know that the truth is: *There is no separation*. There is no *distance* between beings. There is only the temporary *human subjective experience* of separation and distance.

Once you learn that you have the freedom to *choose* your thoughts and feelings, then you can begin to work with the feeling of separation that comes automatically with your "human-hood," so to speak.

If you did nothing, if you did not work with your thoughts and feelings, if you did not reach out to others in love, then the isolation would seem to you to be a *fact*. You would most likely say that it is a reality that comes with your body, with your brain, with your physiological structure. However, if you work creatively with the temporary illusion of separation that you have agreed to live by as a single human, you can eventually peer through to the underlying *eternal connectedness* of all beings. Then, you will be mastering a very large aspect of human joy. The more that you *feel* the truth of love-connectedness beneath the temporary illusion of separation, the more joy you will experience in your life.

❖

You might have noticed that most humans, in all generations, and in all societies, make *marriage*—not because they consciously say, "We must populate the earth by procreating," but, because there can be such joy in that loving union with another human being.

Most ones make families, communities, cities, nations, because they are instinctively searching for that deep joy of *connectedness*. They long to regain the truth that there is no separation. They long to experience once again, as they did in the *beginning* of human life on earth, that all beings are united by forces that you could consider to be *the love of God Itself*.

There can also be some joy in privacy, when it pleases you. But, if you desire love and you are *too* private, then privacy will not please you enough. On the other hand, if you desire privacy and you are intruded upon by others, that will not please you. To balance this area, you could say, "Generally, connectedness brings joy, unless I wish privacy. Then it intrudes." This addresses the complexity of you ones, a complexity that makes it difficult to have joy consistently. In one moment, you desire connectedness and it brings you joy. In another moment, you wish to push it away, feeling that it is an intrusion upon you that will diminish your joy.

These are areas that you ones must understand if you wish more joy in your life. This is part of the freedom and the flexibility needed to have more joy, even when your situation, your desires, your interests *change*.

You might have noticed that in certain marriage areas, there is often change. First, there comes great passion, romance, love. Marriage is very joyful. Then, after a few years, there can come animosity, resentment, and divorce, which is not so joyful. In the beginning of the relationship, you might say, "This marriage one is the key to my joy. I *must* have this one for the remainder of my lifetime to have joy." Then, perhaps, after a few years, you might say, "This mating one is the key to my misery. I *must* be rid of this one or I cannot have joy." It is obvious here that there is *change*. The more rigid that you are, the more you will fail to master in freedom because you do not adjust creatively to the change.

In the *outer* areas of your life where you seek joy in the physical world, you must creatively adjust to change. Imagine that you have a new auto. It is so wonderful and beautiful. It brings you such joy. Seven years later, the auto is dirty and dented. It does not bring you joy. Change has occurred.

In areas of experience in the outer world, when you find certain expressions, experiences, choices that bring you joy, then celebrate. When you notice that those areas no longer bring you joy, then understand that you must make change. You must do something different, make different choices in the outer world, in order to create joy.

A great deal of joy is smothered because a one will stubbornly fasten upon a person, an object, an experience, and say, "This is what I *must* have for joy." They achieve it, but then they hold so tightly that the joy vanishes. They are not bringing forth the flexibility and creativity to move on to the next stage of attaining joy, which requires something different.

The human changeability, in interaction with the outer world of people, places, and things, will drive you ones ever onward. For, what brings you joy in the outer world can become small in a moment. So, you must keep making changes, adding new experiences, in order to create more joy in your life.

❖

Now, there are deeper areas that can *always* bring you joy: *The love that is God. The experience of Divine connectedness.* However, for most ones, these are usually more difficult to achieve than joy in the outer human world. Yet, you can learn to achieve these by practicing with "smaller" areas.

Let us say that you wish to join a tournament of

the golfing, but, you have never played the golf. If you go forth immediately into a tournament, you cannot win. So, you practice in small stages and small games. Then, gradually, you learn to win in the larger areas.

If you would say, "In one single moment I wish to have the joy of experiencing the larger area of Divine Love," you would have difficulty because you have not practiced in the "smaller" area of the joy of simply being you, of loving others, of loving life on earth. It is difficult to immediately leap to the larger levels of experiencing the joy of Divine Love when you have not practiced in the smaller areas of daily joy.

However, we say to you that each of you has often practiced creating joy in the experience of the Divine *before* this lifetime. You are not a blank slate in this area, so, it does not take too long to follow intuition and creative impulses, and indeed examples shown by other humans, to learn what brings joy in the simpler experiences of life, in the more "temporal" experiences. Then, if you are inclined toward the Divine, you can take those kinds of inner shiftings of feelings where you have learned to be joyful because you have this friend, or this activity— and you know what joy feels like—then, with certain adjustments, and a stimulation of your intuitive-sensing-ability, you can take that experience of creating joy in your daily life and willfully turn it toward the Divine in your own way. And, after a period of practice in the silence, you can gradually learn to feel the joy of experiencing Divine Love.

An experience of Divine Love is the only steady focus that will *always* bring you joy. Most other areas of your life will "wear out" over time, or become familiar and less joyful with repetition. That is why, for consistent, ongoing joy in your ordinary daily life, you need to be flexible, adaptable to change, creative in responding to areas that you "wear out." You need to re-stimulate those areas. Along with that, if you wish, you can keep practicing aligning with Divine Love to expand your joy in life.

❖

The "wearing out" of experiences that bring you joy at first, but then dull with repetition, is related to the human "animal" nature associated with your physical body. The constant desire for more and more fulfillment that is an aspect of satisfying bodily needs also influences your desire for more and more fulfilling inner experiences.

Let us say that you love to eat the pork, but you have been trained that you must not eat pork. So, you lust after the pork. Then, you decide to eat it. It is so delicious, and you have an inner experience of joy as you savor eating the pork. The next day, you eat pork again, and your inner experience is a bit less joyful. After many days of continuously eating the pork, you are not interested in the pork. You desire some other kind of food.

So, the animal nature of your physical body will

prod you ones, throughout this lifetime, to always desire *more*, to make changes, to go here, to go there, seeking more fulfillment for your body, which helps you create inner experiences of joy.

When you can experience the pure joy of Divine Love, you never grow tired of that and hunger for something else. The joy of that experience never wears out. It never becomes boring or old. It is always the extraordinarily fulfilling experience of your eternal nature. It is always *perfect* in its nature, even though, at times, your experience of it can fluctuate in intensity and clarity.

So, you can say to yourself, "In my pursuit of joy, I will awaken to the fact that there are two levels of joy. There is the human animal joy of experiences on earth attained through my physical body in interaction with the *outer* world, and, there is the Divine joy of experiencing Divine Love attained within my *inner* experience."

If you have only one of these, it will be difficult to fulfill *completely*. Even Divine Joy without human joy would not be a full mastery of human life on earth. If you learn to attain both, to the best of your ability, you will fulfill. You will master the human world. Most of you understand this in terms of learning, growing, but, you have not yet understood it fully in terms of *joy*.

Most of you have made a promise before you came into earth that, in this lifetime, you will try to live as joyfully and as fully in your physical nature as you will in your Divine nature. So, if you have, for example, a strong sexual desire, you would not tend to fulfill that at the expense of others. You would not fulfill with selfishness and insensitivity. Most likely, to the best of your ability, you would try to bring forth kindness, compassion, and love toward others, which is a Divine impulse, as you integrate with your physical human pleasure.

The key to *full* joy, then, is *enough* of each. If you have too little of one side—the human or the Divine—it diminishes the joy of your life. Therefore, when you are making a plan for experiencing more joy in your life, you need to establish a plan for how much you will embrace the human and how much you will embrace the Divine. Only *you* can say what is best to do to achieve the best balance. And, the balance between the human and the Divine can shift from day to day, according to your shifting situations in the world.

Imagine that you are quite poor and you must work hard at an employment for many hours each day. You come home and you are exhausted. You go to sleep. The next day, you rise up and you go to work again. You do this day after day. Then, you begin to condemn yourself for not focusing upon the Divine. That is not beneficial. You would need to say, "For the moment, I will have no meditation, attunement, or prayer, for I am too busy." That is the cycle that you are presently living and you need to respect it. In the future, you can make some changes in your balance between the human and the Divine.

You ones can say in each day, "How much will I pay attention to my soul today? How much to my physical body? How much to my affairs in earthly life?" The joy comes, not from constantly striving to be absolutely perfect, but from feeling free to do what *you* believe is best to do each day to attain that delicious sense of mastery. *You* are the master of your human *self. You* will decide what is best, and you need to follow your confident choices to the best of your ability.

❖

For the moment, let us show you ones a final area of joy. This has to do with a certain predisposition toward *perfection*. This will vary in all humans. Each of you will have your own particular sense of what is perfect in life, whether you can say it clearly to yourself in thoughts or not. And, when you do not have *enough* perfection—according to your vision of what is perfect—then you will have *less joy*.

If you would go for a long period of time con-stantly saying, "It would be *perfect* to have enough money to make a journey to foreign lands," but, you do not have the money, then you would feel very sad because you cannot do that. You have defined perfection as such a journey, and you feel that you cannot have joy without that journey. Yet, even though you cannot achieve the *perfection* that you see by taking that journey, you can have at least *some* fulfillment of your vision of perfection. You can cease demanding *full* perfection in order to experience joy.

In this example, you can begin to create "small" fulfillments by envisioning activities that you *can* do, and you define *them* as perfect. You might say, "It would be *perfect* to take a walk in the forest." Then, you do that, and now you can have some joy without waiting until you have the money to visit foreign lands. You have created some joy by redefining you vision of "perfection."

You could understand this as working with a desire-fulfillment "ratio." There are certain areas that you ones will define as *perfect*, and the more of those that you can do, even partially, the more joy you will have. When you are deprived of a great deal of those areas, then you can have a challenge with sadness and frustration, and there will be less joy. As desired "perfection" experiences are achieved, the joy goes up, and, as those experiences are blocked, the joy goes down.

❖

For this moment, begin to understand that you have come into this lifetime *to awaken to joy*. You have not come to eliminate flaws in you in order to have more joy. You have come to have the great joy of awakening to your own magnificence as a being.

In this lifetime, you will make certain adjustments in your different inner patterns, and, you will learn about your many complexities. But, if you cannot see the true magnificence of *you*, then most of those adjustments will be temporary. The joy in your life will be fleeting.

So, you might say that the most important key to experiencing joy, for the moment, is: *Seeing the true magnificence within your present human self.* That becomes a foundation upon which you can build more fulfilling experiences as you work with the complexity of your thoughts, feelings, and choices day by day.

For this moment, imagine that all of the complex areas that we have discussed are mastered perfectly. Thus, all that is left to give your attention to is seeing more of your magnificence as a human. This means that you ignore all old thoughts and feelings of limit.

As we now pour forth our love upon you, let there come a willingness to simply see, *within you,* a bright, and beautiful, and shining magnificence that is your true nature. In this moment, let yourself feel that nothing—no thought, no feeling, no experience—can change or diminish that magnificence. That is the eternal perfection of God Itself that lives within you.

For this moment, as we are loving you, create that feeling, that vision, that inner sensing of the brilliance, beauty, goodness, and magnificence of *you.* Know that this is the key that you have been searching for. It is the foundation upon which you can build so much joy, day by day, throughout this lifetime.

And, for this time in earth, the speaking is ended.

❖ ❖ ❖

CHAPTER 2

The Second Reading

The Guides' Opening Teaching

We would look now at the capacity of you ones to make *a freedom from pressure*. When you do that, you open the way for much greater joy in your life. But, each individual would have differences in their inner tendencies and capacities to make this adjustment.

Imagine that you have qualified for running in an important race. *Theoretically*, you have the *potential* to win, no matter how many good runners are in the race. You have the "equipment" to win a race. You have legs. You have feet. You have a body that can run. But, *practically*, you will run slow, or you will run fast, in alignment with many of your *personal* complexities, including your health, your training, your experience in racing, and many other personal factors.

In the same way, theoretically, you ones all have the equipment—the makeup—of a Divine Being who is temporarily expressing in a human form. This is equivalent to having a body to race. But, in practicality, in terms of actually winning the race—meaning that your present human *self* will *fully* manifest the power of joy—there are differences amongst you ones in the likelihood of achieving that.

Some of you, in this lifetime, have been quite severely berated by others, and pushed down by negative circumstances. Some have suffered from dramatic negative family experiences, or painful broken love relationships.

Others carry great dreads as non-conscious patterns from past lifetimes of earth that would cause them to say, in effect, "I dare not let down my guard. I must always be alert for the dangers of earth life." For some of you, in the past lifetimes, this is related to physical attacks upon your body, or political danger in certain lifetimes—various human experiences in the past in which, if you *did* let down your guard, if you were not cautious, guarded, suspicious, protected in dangerous situations, you might have been captured and put into death.

We are showing you this so that if you feel that you are a one who has been beaten down, emotionally speaking, by various negative circumstances in this lifetime, or, if you have carried a consistent sense of dread, or feelings of danger, or pressure, or limit, you can see this as a guardedness that you have brought from past lifetimes of earth to heal in this lifetime. Thus, you can understand why you might need to say, "It is more difficult for me to win the race of joy in this lifetime."

That feeling is quite understandable. But, it is simply *a temporary feeling*, and you must remember that you are a Divine Being expressing in human form. You have the equipment to win the race with more practice and training.

You can understand negative tendencies from past lifetimes as patterns that *you-as-a-soul* have chosen for your present human *self* to learn from and master in this lifetime. In the mastering of those challenging patterns, you bring forward your full strength and power to run even faster in the race of attaining the fullness of joy in this lifetime.

❖

If you are not one of the rare individuals who has an innate tendency to always be a joyful, happy person, then you could say, "Joy is somewhat of a challenge for me. I need to pay more attention to joy, laughter, playfulness, aliveness, than those who do not have my particular challenge patterns." And, you would understand that *you-as-a-soul* have chosen those challenge patterns that tend to block joy, so, you are not inadequate or lacking because you have those patterns. You are simply learning to master those patterns, and, as you master them, you open the way for more and more joy in your life.

No matter what challenge patterns you ones are working with that block your joy, there are certain keys that you can use effectively to guide yourself. We will point to these areas, and, if you will remember them and use them each day, you will find that your capacity for joy—the deep underlying capacity that is your *true potential*, your Divine "equipment"—can be brought forward, no matter what your present relationship to joy might be.

❖

The **first key** is to convince yourself, by use of your own powerful thoughts, that *there is no danger to your being in this lifetime.*

Of course, there can be danger to your physical body. If you are walking in a dark alleyway and there are violent robbers lurking about, there is a danger to your body. But, *you* are not your body. If you are attacked, even murdered, *you are not diminished in your being.* You would simply make another death and you would move forward to more of the unfolding of the grand drama of human life on earth.

So, this first key to greater joy is to spend some time each day "detaching" from the human life in the physical world to make a loving silent attunement. In the silence, you would say to yourself:

> "*I am an eternal soul.* No matter how serious my challenges might appear in the moment, they are all *temporary.* Loneliness is temporary. Poverty is temporary. Illness is temporary. *All challenges are temporary.*"

Then, you can say to yourself:

> "I am *eternal.* I outlive all challenges. Throughout this life, and in death, *nothing can damage or diminish my being.*"

When you are not making this attunement, you will not "detach." You will need to work honestly with your doubts and fears—to fully experience them, live through them, then release them. But, each day, you need that gentle silent period in which you attune to the eternal nature of your being in this way that we have suggested.

It would be very beneficial to make this attunement as soon as you awaken from your sleeping place. You would enter the silence and fasten upon the deeper truth of you by saying:

> "I am a permanent eternal being. But, as a human temporarily expressing in the physical world, I will live this coming day as much as possible with a passion, with a feeling of great freedom, even a sense of invulnerability. I may be caused some emotional pain. My body can be caused harm. Yet, it is all temporary. So, I will try to take this day lightly, even playfully. I will try to smile at my own foibles. I will live honestly with my challenging thoughts and feelings, and try to share them and vent them. That will relieve some pressure upon me. But, even if I do not do that, even if I have years of misery on earth, that cannot damage my being. It is all temporary. I am *eternal*."

This is similar to having an assignment in a stage drama. You are the theatrical acting one. At times, you must play in the dramas that are tragedies. And, during the play, to achieve the masterful performance, you could be frightened, sad, or you might temporarily live in despair. You are so good at playing the role that you forget that it is a play. You are *living* the drama, and it very is frightening and troubling.

You give a wonderful performance. Then, the play ends. You realize that you have lived *through* temporary negativity and now it is over. And, as you repeat the play night after night, even though you must fully live the negativity each time, with experience, you come to trust that it is all temporary. So, beneath the drama, you can feel a certain light-heartedness. You do not take the drama so seriously, but, you still play it out fully and completely.

Each day, you wish to be serious about your desires, your interests, your concerns, your fulfillments, your challenges of human life. Yet, when you remember that it is all temporary, and it is not dangerous to your being, then your fear in life is lessened and you open the door to more joy.

❖

The **second key** to more joy and happiness in your life is to find certain ways to approach other humans that are not in the context of *a push and pull.* The reason that you ones can more easily rejoice in loved ones is that, generally, you are not competing with them. You are not combating. You are not threatening one another. Most of the time, you ones will be calm and trusting with loved ones, family, and friends.

Some will be apprehensive with strangers. Yet, once they come to know a stranger and there is friendship, the apprehension, or protectiveness falls away.

The protectiveness is quite "natural," since you ones have lived in earth so many times, and, in a number of lifetimes, certain humans have not been kind to you. In fact, some in the past lifetimes have been quite cruel, and they have mistreated you strongly. Some of you, even in this lifetime, have had that experience.

So, you might say that it is natural to approach "stranger-humans," and those not familiar to you, not yet befriended, with a certain sense of protectiveness. And, this protectiveness grows as a shell. Through the years, it becomes stiffer, unless you practice peeling away layers of it.

Even if you are working wonderfully in all other areas to create joy in your life, the sense of going into the world of strangers can influence you to carry the shell of protectiveness about you, which increases feelings of threat, danger, seriousness. All of that makes it more difficult to take your daily moments lightly, and to feel that there is laughter and play in your experiences. You are temporarily unable to feel that your human life is a grand and glorious *adventure*, not a battleground.

This area needs to be thought through carefully. You need to notice how you go forth toward strangers, particularly those who might be unkind and insensitive. With such ones, you may *need* to be a bit guarded to make certain that you do not unnecessarily expose yourself too much to those who are unkind. But, most ones in your environment will not wish to attack you, or compete with you. And, usually, if you are willing to be the first one to show the warmth, the friendship, and the light, playful attitude, most strangers—unless they are deeply confused—will respond in kind. This is how you can have more sense of lightness and playfulness in your social life with strangers.

With loved ones and friends—those that you generally are willing to be relaxed with, and trust, and not feel that you must protect against them—usually, the joy is diminished by challenging situations and complexities in the relationship that make it difficult to laugh and play.

Let us say that you have a wonderful mating one. In general, there is love between you ones, but, you have many complexities in your relationship with one another in your daily life. You ones fret so much about the complexities that you argue and squeeze the joy out of being together. You need not try to force the challenges away, but, you can decide: If human life on earth is so short, and if you wish to laugh and play with your mating one, do you wish to spend your entire day fussing and fretting about complexities—pushing, pulling, competing, being tense, and bickering—those areas. Or, do you wish to remember that those complexities *are created by yourselves*, and, *they can be released by yourselves*.

It would take a bit of patient practice to communicate more fully, and to release the complexities of criticism and fault-finding, in order to open the way to joy. Particularly in the marriage areas and in the love areas, fault-finding and a lack of communication are the most predominant heavy forces that squeeze the joy out of the relationship.

Another factor for those who are less enlightened in working with the complexities in the relationship area, particularly in the mating relationships, is a feeling that would say, "This is not the right relationship for me. This one does not bring me enough joy." When, it may be that you ones are actually sabotaging your own joy by over-serious fretting, fussing, competing, pushing, pulling—all of those areas.

These are complex, difficult areas for many ones, but, they are very strong pivotal points, in terms of creating joy, play, laughter in your relationships with others, particularly in a mating relationship.

❖

The **third key** is to look at the area that you ones would call "fun." Let us say that you come into a room where there is a grand celebration by many ones. There is singing, dancing, cavorting. Many are there having the strong freedom feeling, the *fun* feeling.

As you come into the room, you expect everyone to come to you and welcome you as one of the prize guests. Instead, as you enter, the hostess approaches you and says to you, "It is your task to clean the room. You will follow ones about and pick up their droppings for the entire evening." Now, your expectations are shattered. You would not say that you are experiencing fun. The *duties*, the *efforts*, the *requirements*, the *demands*, are not fun.

Then, imagine that, in the very same example, you come forth *knowing* that you are the hired cleaning person. And, you know that you will be paid a great deal of money for the cleaning. Now, it *is* fun, for there is a great sense of goodness about the monies that you will receive. You might even find a bit of joy in performing the duties.

In the important human area of *fun*, first, you need to understand how you see it. What seems to be fun to you, and what is not fun? You need to clarify what kind of attitudes, thoughts, feelings, expectations, interests, desires—all of those areas—that you bring toward the area of fun.

As you analyze your individual patterns, keep in mind that the "fun factor" is often dependent upon *newness*. Let us say that each day you come to a joyful party as a guest. The next day, you come to the same party. And, the next day, and the next day, and, for forty-seven days, you come to the same party. Now, it is not as much fun because there is no newness in the experience.

Fun also has to do with your *expectations* about an event or an experience. With something that is fun for you, there is usually not a *demand* for you to do it. You do not expect it to be a repulsive duty, or something that is oppressive. Your expectation is that it is something that is playful, or new, or inviting in some way. It has no burden to it. And, you expect that it will not be repetitive to the point of boredom, or numbness to the joy factor.

Imagine that you would say, "I take joy in petting frogs. It is fun to have pet frogs." You buy several frogs and you have some fun with them. Then, you buy some more frogs and you have more fun. Then, you decide, "I love frogs so much that I will have a frog shop for a business." Now, you must *sell* frogs.

Imagine that in your business you do not sell enough frogs. Your business fails and you have poverty. Now, you have no fun with the frogs. They are now a burden. The activity that was fun for you is now bringing you frustration and negative feelings.

This illustrates the need to be constantly creative and alert to *changing patterns* in the activities that bring you fun. You need to *refresh* those activities when they grow weak in their ability to stimulate fun for you.

Another factor in the fun area is *spontaneity*. Imagine that you plan a journey to the land of Italy. You fret and fuss about the details of the journey trying to make it perfect. As you carry out the journey, you bring forth a sense of strong control and manipulation of everything you do in the Italy, trying to make it perfect. From that, you might have a bit of fun, but, generally, you are exhausted from your overly-rigid efforts that have controlled the journey to the point where there is no spontaneity at all in your experience.

When you say, "I need some areas of fun in my life," first, identify what seems to be fun for you. If you have no sense of that, you might need to refer to others to see what they believe is fun. Usually, this would be *play* of some type.

Then, you try out the chosen area. If you find that you are desperately forcing yourself to have fun, then that might not be the best area for you. But, if your experience is light, and playful, and there is no pressure, and it is done simply for fun, not for profit, or to make yourself more perfect, then you have a wonderful area to enjoy. Over a period of time, if it is no longer fun for you, then you can change to some other area.

Now, you ones must be cautious here, for, often, to some, the "forbidden" areas seem to be the most fun—forbidden by society, or by your own morals, or by your sense of what is healthy for your body. You must use some intelligence here. But, once you decide, "Here is an area that is fun for me, it is not detrimental to my health, to my morals, to my standing in society, it is not illegal," then, you can pursue it with a wonderful sense of freedom, a sense of playfulness, and release, and joy. You would pursue it as often as you wish, while you continue on in the other important areas of your life that, at times, are not so much fun, but they need to be accomplished in order to keep attaining what is important to you.

In your daily human experience, there are usually some "restrictions" to how much time you can spend having fun. For most of you, you must spend quite a bit of time working to earn enough money to sustain yourself in the physical world. Some must work in areas that are not particularly aligned with their creativity, and their deeper talents and abilities, so, some can feel burdened by the working arena. Thus, it can be difficult for them to have fun in their daily activities.

If you feel that, for the financial reward, you must continue in a present occupation that is not fulfilling, know that you have the inner capacity to make it more interesting. You have the capacity to awaken your creativity to engage every working moment more fully. If you were in your working arena knowing that you had but one final day to be alive in this lifetime, one day to see the persons, to do the activities—one final day to be your present human *self*—you could make that a most *precious* day. You could savor every touch, every action of your work, that earlier seemed to be a burden. You could have a sense of playfulness, and joy, and even fun.

Each day, remind yourself:

"The very forces of God Itself that have created this entire universe live within my human *self*. Certainly, with those extraordinary energies available to me in my thoughts, feelings, and choices, I have enough power and potency to create joy in any moment, even in moments that seem less than perfect to me."

❖

The **fourth key** to wielding the power of joy in your life is the establishment of a framework in daily life in which you take time to *put aside the human path.* No matter how sensitive, creative, intelligent, sincere, dedicated to truth you are, one single day of "being human" can be exhausting, particularly in the present complexity of the human world in which you ones live. So, you need a period of at least five or ten moments in each day in which you *cease engaging* the human world.

This takes a bit of practice. In the silent moments, you must practice ignoring all thoughts and feelings about your present human pathway, even the very positive areas that you are attaining. It needs to be as though those things did not exist. During the silence, you will practice feeling that you are not your present human *self.* You will practice feeling that you are an eternal soul.

One way to playfully "shock" yourself into releasing the human pathway during this silent period is to imaginatively practice experiencing your death. Each day, for five or ten moments, sit in the silence, calm yourself, and say to yourself, "It is time to make death. In this moment, I no longer care about money, clothing, health, the physical world. All I care about is this extraordinary Divine Love that I am now becoming aware of as I release the physical world. I realize that while I was busy living my human life, I did not fully experience this love because of the distractions of the physical world. Now, since I am making death, all of those areas fall away, and I can clearly feel the Divine Love lifting me. I can feel the eternal souls embracing me, celebrating me, and rejoicing in my return home."

This kind of practice in the silence you might call a "spiritual practice." But, it is also an awakening to Divine Joy. At times, you could say, "I do this to awaken to my soul, to God." At other times, you could say, "I do this to have Divine Joy."

❖

These are some focal points that you ones can use to awaken the healing power of joy in your life. You will also discover other ways from your own thoughts, feelings, and personal experience.

As you work diligently with the focal points each day, not only will you begin to experience more joy in your life, but, you will also find that you are aligning more and more with an experience of being an eternal soul who is temporarily expressing a portion of your Divine Consciousness as the wonderful human *self* that is you in this present lifetime.

❖

Questions and Answers

Note: During this five-day retreat, there were numerous questions asked by the participants that were answered by the Guides. Many of those questions pertained only to the personal issues of the individuals in the retreat group, and they are kept private. Only the questions and answers that have teaching value for everyone are included in this book.

The woman who asked the following question felt that her habit of working hard to achieve in life made it difficult for her to take time for joy. The Guides' answer to her question can be helpful to anyone who feels that they are too busy to bring joy into their daily life.

QUESTION ONE: I have a tendency to view life like I am a warrior and life is a battle. It's very difficult for me to take the attitude that life is a play or a dance. It's very ingrained in me that while I am here on earth I've got these goals, and I've got things that I want to do. It's like I've come to do battle and that seems important to me. I feel like it would be frivolous for me to take the attitude that dance, and play, and laughter are important. I need some help in gaining that new perspective. If I do switch my perspective, how would that benefit me personally?

THE GUIDES: As you can understand, you must begin with a kind of tolerant, amused acceptance of your present "warrior" patterns, for certainly there is no fault in them. There is no flaw in you. There is simply less joy.

You could say to yourself, "The adjustment in my perspective can be very gradual. I will not give up my strong desires, my interests, my fulfilling of needs, my protecting when I feel I must." All of that will continue as it is.

It is as though you are driving a herd of buffalo. You must take them to a distant city to the southeast. As you are driving steadily day after day, you become so obsessed with not veering even one degree from your direction that the entire journey is filled with tension. You arrive at your destination with great success in delivering your buffalo, but, because of your constant over-striving to do it so perfectly, you have had no joy in the journey.

If, on the journey, you would have said, "I will always move the herd southeast, but, a small deflection here and there can be easily corrected," then you could have enjoyed the journey. In other words, you can allow small lapses of what you consider to be *responsibility* and *duty*. You can even allow a small self-indulgence in pleasing yourself at times instead of perfectly accomplishing every task. That experience brings forth a feeling of freedom and joy. Then, whenever you wish, you can return again to your diligent pursuit of your goals.

You can begin to see the change in small increments, where you practice being a bit less cautious, or less ambitious, or less fulfilling of duties, or less responsible. Then, you can have a taste of what you previously would have mistakenly called "irresponsibility," or "selfishness," or "laziness."

As you taste this new freedom in small doses, you will discover that you do not suddenly become a bad person if you indulge in your own pleasure, play, and laughter from time to time. You will realize that you are still the wonderful human being that you were when you were over-striving to do everything perfectly. You will see that you are a wonderful human when you are pleasing yourself, when you are doing what you might have previously *thought* was self-indulgent, or even selfish. With these small doses of play and laughter, you learn to be more relaxed and more free, then you can bring that forward while you are pursuing the important goals and achievements that you have for yourself in this lifetime.

As a one who loves to serve others, there are other factors here which have to do with a difficulty of *receiving from others*. Thus, in general, you have not received enough appreciation from others. You have not had enough of the feeling of joy that comes from being celebrated by others. You lack the experience of seeing how wonderful you appear in the eyes of others, which could strongly boost your confidence and help you feel that you are truly wonderful.

If you had the full experience of being appreciated by others, then, you would not have the impulse to *prove* how wonderful you are by constantly being perfect in your duties, your achievements. You would have more leeway, be more relaxed, more flexible, and you would have the opportunity for the herd of buffalo to drift a bit, even while it is still moving in the direction that you have set.

The receiving from others is very important, but, when you think about this area, it stirs some old patterns in you that would be a fear to ask others to give to you. You have a fear to be too "needy," and a fear to be rejected by others if you are seen as needy.

It can be helpful to understand that even after you have reached certain goals by over-striving, the *habit* of fussing and fretting to be perfect will continue. Imagine that you attain wealth, perfect marriage, beautiful home, wonderful life. Now, you are joyful for a while. Then, you notice that you have a challenge with a friend. You feel that you are not perfect enough to the friend. You do not have perfect thoughts. You are critical. Then, you notice that you begin to be frightened about losing your wealth. You then continue to struggle emotionally even after you have reached your goals. So, you might say, "Perhaps *before* I reach my goals, I can heal the habit of fussing, and fretting, and trying too hard in life to reach those goals. Then, I can be joyful *before* I reach my goals. And, I will be more joyful after I reach them."

As you work lovingly with your old habits here, you will notice that your patterns show a great deal of loosening, and expanding, and, there will be more trusting. It is simply a matter of continuing the daily observing of your patterns, noticing the old ones that are a bit too strict, and deciding how to loosen them.

Then, always, it is a matter of receiving more from the humans around you. You might specify more activities that have to do with fun and play with others in which there is more opportunity to receive goodness from them.

Also, each day, actively seek out experiences that you can do simply for the joy of it, remembering that human life is so short, and you would not wish to spend it all in constant effort and work.

❖

NOTE: One way that spiritual seekers tap into the power of joy is to create an experience of the souls who guide them in their life. In previous Readings, the Guides have said that each person has a small group of "spiritual guides." In the following question, a woman asks about her personal guides. She is given a potent way to envision those guides. The answer to her question can help everyone gain a sense of how to experience their spiritual guides, which can be a major step in opening to the power of joy.

QUESTION TWO: In a Reading not too long ago, you told me that I have three spiritual guides. Would you please tell me more about them? What my guides' names might be? Why might we have chosen to be together this time around? And what particular thing are we working on? Have we shared any prior lives together?

THE GUIDES: When you look at this area, you can imagine that you are a horse, running in a herd of wild horses. Then, imagine that you are captured by a farmer, trained, and you must plow the fields. There would be a *harness* to attach you to the plow.

In the same way, you need certain "constraints" in the human experience in order to keep your consciousness from "vacating" your physical body. Without those constraints, there could be a complete detachment from your human mental, emotional, and physical patterns. That detachment would enable you to fully satisfy your desire for an experience of the Divine, but it would prevent you from mastering your human life on earth.

You have felt the "harness" throughout this lifetime. And, given your passion for the Divine, for perfection, for God, the harness has felt a bit tight at times. But, you have plowed quite well.

You might say that now it is time to occasionally take off the harness and indulge a bit in your desire for greater conscious awareness of the Divine in order to experience the extraordinary joy that such an experience can bring you. And, a focus upon the souls that you would consider to be your *guiding souls*, can be one of the areas that will help you have more fulfillment, in terms of experiencing the Divine, experiencing these souls.

The challenge here is that, if you would say, "Speak of a name and a personality for each of my guiding ones," you are putting back on the harness. You are limiting yourself by *human thought* and *human perceptions rooted in physical reality*. Yet, if you do not have *some* human thoughts and perceptions, then your guiding souls remain invisible to you.

So, let us suggest a structure that you can use *lightly*, so that you do not over-think about this area. This structure can stimulate your imagination so that when you make a silent attunement to your guiding souls, you have a place to begin.

In other words, if you are simply attuning to Divine *vastness*, it is similar to attempting to climb a mountain without any footholds. You simply slip backward. But, if there are small niches in the mountain, and you put your fingers in them, you can climb up bit by bit. However, you do not say, "These niches are the whole mountain." They are simply niches—small parts of the mountains. We will show you some niches, some hand-holds, for climbing the mountain of Divine Reality to become aware of your guiding souls. And, remember that the vision that we give you is not the full reality of those souls.

First, when you think of your guiding souls, think in terms of three *perfect* Divine Beings. Whenever you make an attunement to them, you can begin by imagining them around you in a triangulation in which you are the wonderful human in the center. These three extraordinary perfect beings stand around you in a triangular formation.

Then, you invite yourself to begin to *feel* their Divine *presence* as a most wonderful feeling of being nurtured, valued, appreciated, and perfectly loved by them.

Then, if you wish to try to give *form* to their presence, you can imagine them as shimmering, glowing beings of such extraordinary beauty that when you imagine a visage, a face, on these beings, the radiant beauty of their countenance touches you to your depths. These are the sweetest, most beautiful, most perfect faces—*angelic* from the human point of view—gleaming, free of all tension and human negativity, filled with pure and perfect light and love.

Now, such images are the niches in the mountain. These are not *the full eternal reality* of these three souls. They are simply some beginning points for your mind and your feelings.

To put *human names* to these souls is a limitation, for naming is a human "tool." If you must name them, then, it does not matter what names you use. You could say to yourself, "I will call them 'one,' 'two,' and 'three.'" No matter what you name them, they are still what they are. But, your naming of them fulfills your need to have a certain *distinguishing* sense so that you can sense them as individual souls.

Thus, in your attunement, when you imagine that you are in the middle of the triangle of these perfect souls, first, you look straight ahead. There is the first guiding soul to you. You can imagine this one as the fullest, most perfect *feminine love*. It is as though this is the most *nurturing* being in the entire universe, in the "mothering" sense. So, straight before you, in the triangle, is the Divine Mother, who would love you even if you decided to commit great negativity in this human life. This is a love that knows no judgment, no criticism, no fault-finding. You could never cause this one to cease loving you.

You have known this particular soul in human form in two previous lifetimes on earth in which her *human* capacity to love you was quite close to this perfect Divine love. If you feel, in time, as you learn to experience the love from this soul, a certain sense of a human *name* that seems to well up from within you, then you might say, "This is the name by which I knew this one as a human before this lifetime."

Then, as you stand in the triangle of the guiding souls, to your right would be the second guiding soul.

As you learn to experience this soul, you will have a sense of stabilizing, steadiness, security, as though you have a perfect father who can master every facet of life and keep you secure from everything. Nothing can shake you as this father stands strong with you. Nothing can defeat this one. This one has perfect courage, and strength, and determination. And, that is woven with a perfect love for you. So, you might say, "Here is the perfect Divine Father." As you learn to experience the presence of this one, a naming might arise within your mind that you feel embodies the wonderful qualities of this soul.

Then, to your left is the third guiding soul. For the moment, in thinking about this niche in the mountain—this small aspect of this particular guiding soul—you could say, "Here is the Divine Child." For this present period of your life, you could say, "This one embodies the perfect child upon which I have often tried to pour my human love as a mother," but a mother in the *largest* sense. Then, this Divine Child feeds back into you such adoration of you as a mother.

This structure gives you a sense of a *flow*, where the first and second guiding souls *pour love into you*, and the third one draws out of you the most wonderful love, and then returns it to you as adulation and appreciation.

Each of these three guiding souls has had a similar role in your life in past human lifetimes, but, there has been much more than this that is the rest of the mountain. However, you cannot climb the mountain in one step, so you need these small steps to begin.

❖

The Guides' Closing Teaching

Let us look now at the *range* of joy that human ones can create in their experience on earth, related to how much you ones *engage life*. This can be seen as a large balloon in which humans fly. It is very full of the hot air, and it is aloft, but, it is tied to the earth by strong ropes.

For those who wish only a small balloon ride—they wish to protect and be safe in life—there is no need to release the ropes. This represents the experience of joy that is simply gained naturally when there is not too much severe challenge in your life. You are not disabled. You are not blind. You are not dying of cancer. You are not being imprisoned and tortured. In other words, simply not having misery brings a certain amount of joy while you go about guarding yourself against the challenges of life. That is the balloon that is tied to the earth, but it is still floating in the air in a small range.

Then, certain human ones have longer lines, but they are still tied to the earth. You are moving about in a larger range. Your doubts and fears are not that heavy, and your sense of awakening is stronger, so you live your life with more freedom and passion. You are more able to have joy, whether your day seems perfect or not.

Then, there are some humans who have no lines at all. You have the capacity to go in all directions as you live your life to the fullest with great *passion* and *emotional engagement*. At times, your balloon may rise to such altitudes that you are buffeted by the strong currents of emotional challenge. That is the choice that you make. You are willing to fully open yourself emotionally to have the freedom, to have the stronger sense of aliveness, joyfulness, playfulness, even though it means that when there is challenge, you will feel the negativity more strongly.

❖

You can notice that in the range of joy that we have given, we have not said that any human has *perfect* joy. In this lifetime, humans will not attain perfect, constant joy. You will have *imperfect* joy, because you are humans living in a complex physical world that makes many demands upon you. But, imperfect joy, attained often at a *high* level is quite wonderful.

Since perfect joy will not be attained, you could say to yourself, "Then I will cease demanding perfect joy. I will continue to rise higher and higher in my sense of freedom, and flexibility, and aliveness, to attain high levels of joy as often as I can. Occasionally, I will be buffeted by winds of worry and doubt, and fear and challenge. That is the price that I pay for being emotionally adventurous. Always, after I live through the negativity, I will return to soaring high above the sense of limitation and I will regain the great joy of being fully alive."

❖

For this moment, focus upon what you desire for this time in your life. Do you desire the more stable, secure balloon that is tied closely to earth? Then, you can have a certain amount of joy, along with less turbulence—less being buffeted by every thought and feeling that comes along. The joy is smaller, but you are willing to accept that in exchange for more predictability, more security. If that feels important to you at this time, then rejoice in that, for no choice is better or worse than the other. There are simply different choices with different results. Whatever you choose, you are still an eternal being.

If, for this moment in your life, you feel that you have been too buffeted by challenge, you could say, "I wish to be tied more closely to the strong, stable foundations of life." Then, that is the approach that you take, for a while. You can always choose a different focus in the future.

If you wish a moderate soaring forth and freedom, you make that your intention for a while. That is how you will guide yourself.

If you desire the fullest experience, then you would say to yourself, "I am strongly believing that even the most terrible mental-emotional experiences cannot damage my being. I love soaring high with intensity, believing in all goodness, trying everything that seems best and good, opening as fully as possible to all ones that I meet, loving them as deeply as I can, even if that opens me to some possible rejection and emotional pain."

Each one must choose their own way. And, the key is to feel that *you have the power to choose.* You have the power to choose the extent of joy, the length of it, the depth of it, how much of it you will stimulate, how much you will not.

❖

With this great sense of power within you in this moment of time, we would ask that you feel that you are rising up as a unique individual human who is expressing the Forces of God. In this moment, say to yourself:

> "*I* am the one who determines my life through my choices. I will make my choices with as much clarity and honesty as possible. Then, after my death, *I-as-a-soul* will rejoice to the fullest in what this human *self* has achieved in this lifetime."

Now, say to yourself:

> "I take the power of God Itself into my hands, and I will wield it each day by the wise choices that I make. I rejoice in my wisdom to make choices that bless myself and those upon this earth."

If you take that as your vision, and as your vow, then you will have the deepest joy possible for you, day by day, throughout this lifetime.

And, for this time in earth, the speaking is ended.

❖ ❖ ❖

CHAPTER 3

The Third Reading

The Guides' Opening Teaching

For the extension of your intellectual understanding of the emotion, the *feeling*, of joy, we would suggest that you understand it as a complex "partnership" between your thoughts and your feelings. For example, if you have a wonderful *thought* of a beloved one, then there can be a *feeling* of joy. If you have a thought of a one who threatens you and challenges you, then you would not expect feelings of joy.

After you work patiently with your thoughts and feelings, then it is time to monitor, and oversee, and, at times adjust, the interaction between your thoughts and your feelings. This adjustment goes in both "directions." If you would have great *feelings* of heaviness, your thoughts might say, "This is wrong," or, "This is bad," or, "I am doomed." In the other direction, if you have the *thought*, "My life is terrible," then you can have the great feeling of heaviness.

The *monitoring* of the complex interaction

between thought and feeling, which most ones simply take for granted, is an important aspect of creating joy. Without the wise monitoring, your thoughts and feelings can "run wild," so to speak, and they can create experiences that do not please you. Eventually, you can become a slave to your habits of thinking and feeling.

As you do this monitoring, it is wise, as most of you would tend to do without noticing, to collect a "repertoire" of thoughts that bring you feelings of joy. Then, you can create those thoughts whenever you wish to have some feelings of joy.

❖

Then, you will need to work with certain thoughts about negative feelings so that you can "feed back" into the emotional area, a kind of refined, *healing impulse* for the negative thoughts.

To clarify this, imagine that you are walking in a beautiful field. You have the thought, "This field is beautiful." Then, you have a feeling of joy in response to your thought and to the beauty that you see in the field. All of that can transpire without much notice from you, but, if you *monitor* that process—without being overly self-conscious and ruining the spontaneity of the moment—you could say, "How wonderful that I have *responded* to this beautiful place in the physical world with a feeling of joy. This reveals to me the power that I have to *create* an experience of joy."

Then, later, you might be creating the thought

that you are inadequate as a person. From that thought, you have a feeling of badness. You can briefly accept that feeling, live through it, then release it.

Then, you would say, "In this moment, it pleases me to oversee the interaction between my thinking and feeling by willfully *choosing* to think about that beautiful field where I felt such joy." As you begin to think about the field, as you fully envision it and you recall the joyful experience of it, then you have initiated feelings of joy to replace the earlier feeling of badness.

These are very simple focal points, but most ones never notice the power and potency of them. This is one of the important keys to wielding the healing power of joy in your life.

So, it is wise to collect a repertoire of thoughts, images, memories that stimulate feelings of joy within you. And, when you are not busy doing something else in your day-to-day life, when you have a moment of freedom, or peacefulness, you can draw upon that reservoir. In this example, you would say, "I choose now to create thoughts of my beautiful field because it brings me a feeling of joy, and that pleases me."

The more that you exercise this freedom to use the interaction between thought and feeling to please yourself by creating some feelings of joy, the more joyful you will become in all areas of your life. As long as you are working honestly with any negative thoughts and feelings that you generate—experiencing them fully, living through them, releasing them—then this choosing to willfully create feelings of joy by working with your thoughts and feelings will serve you well throughout your life.

❖

Now, in the understanding that you are gaining of the healing power of joy, the next area to examine closely is: The thoughts that you have about *yourself*. You can understand that not only do negative thoughts about you fail to bring you joy, but, they can bring you feelings of misery.

If you would think, "I am so inadequate as a person, I am so unloved, I will never be fully loved," those thoughts, when indulged in for long periods of time without being fully experienced, shared, and vented, will squeeze the joy out of your life. This can occur even if you have happy circumstances and ones are loving you quite well. These kinds of thoughts of *self-diminishment* rob you of joy.

As you might expect, thoughts of your true magnificence as a human *self* can *stimulate* feelings of joy.

So, in wielding the power of joy, *the attitude that you take toward yourself*—as in many areas of your life—is a very important focal point, in terms of how much joy you will have in this lifetime. You can see quite clearly that the more you use thoughts to criticize and condemn yourself, the less joy you will have. The more your thoughts fasten upon the truth of you as a wonderful human *self*, the more joy you will have in your life. The more you will be able to play, and sing, and dance, and laugh.

In the interaction between thought and feeling, you have only to observe your habits of self-diminishment thoughts and you will see clearly what they do to your feelings.

Then, there are certain *feelings* that you can invite that can cause you to think, "How wonderful I am." When you create feelings of purpose and meaning about what you do in life, then you can think about what a good person you are. Cultivate and collect these kinds of thoughts and feelings. Notice the interaction between the two, and make choices that bring you more joy in managing that interaction.

❖

Most of you can understand that the physical body that you inhabit is similar to a beautiful auto, in that it comes forth quite new, and, for most of you, intact, functioning well. Then, it begins to wear out. It has chipped paint, and there are dents, and it grows weak in its performance.

In the same way, there are various aspects of the human body that respond to many factors in your world. Those factors either move you toward strength and health on the one hand, or, illness and debilitation on the other.

These factors in your world are very complex, and there are many of them. In terms of bringing more joy into the experience of you, and then, having benefit from the joy in the health of your physical body, it can be important to have at least some simple thoughts and understandings of these complex factors. Be aware that there are many complexities here that we will *not* speak about for the moment.

To guide yourself in the very simplest way of thinking, you could say, "The more joy that I have in this life, the more benefit there will be to my physical body."

Now, the opposite of this is not exactly true. You could have a great deal of the opposite of joy—which is sadness, pain, misery—and if you share those negative experiences fully with sensitive ones, live through them, release them, then there would be very little detriment to the health of your body. So, you might say that—again in a simple way—joy is *healing* for your body, but, the absence of joy, and the presence of temporary negative thoughts and feelings, is not necessarily illness-causing, unless you swallow the negative thoughts and feelings on a consistent basis over a period of time.

❖

It can be beneficial now to approach a few of the complexities that have to do with the way in which joy, and the celebration of life, can benefit the health of your physical body. The first understanding can be focused on the mysterious *blood activity* of the human body. It is not by accident that the blood has been extremely important in ancient understandings of human life.

Within your present human body, there is a *being*. That being expresses as the temporary *human-self-energy-structure* that gives you the experience of being *you*. There is a very deep link between this *non-physical* human *self* and the *physical* body. That link involves a kind of "threshold" through which invisible *non-physical energies* must pass in order to become *physical*.

At the "smallest" level, this would occur in the "particles of matter" that you ones have a fondness for naming in a scientific manner. These are the atoms and the "sub-atomic" particles that are so fascinating to many of you ones.

In the smallest *physical* structure, the smallest "particle" reality that ones can actually *perceive*—not *theorize* about—there is a kind of *mystical process* in which, that which is *eternal* and Divine *outside* of time and space, becomes *temporal* and physical *inside* of time and space. You might imagine a mystical "transforming portal" through which, what you would call "energies," will pass to become first, tangible physical "sub-atomic" particles, then the physical matter of which the physical world is made.

Now, the only reason that you need this under-standing is that this mystical transformation process occurs *in your blood*. Literally, it occurs in the blood cells within your body. You could say that the blood cells are the "first" cells to receive the "artifact" of this mystical transformation in which non-physical

Divine energy is transformed into finite physical energy, and then into physical matter in the form of the molecules that make up the cells of your blood.

Putting aside the physiological processes for the moment, understand that what is important here is to know that the blood is the first threshold through which the Divine Forces pass to become your body. This occurs "beneath" your physiology—beneath the biological functioning of your body.

Then, for your purposes, you would need to say, "If I have sadness and pain for long periods, and I do not share my negative feelings, and I do not have comfort from others, and there is not enough joy in my life for a long period of time, then, there begins a process of "contamination" of the inflowing of Divine Forces that rejuvenate the blood cells of my body." Those blood cells you might think of as *the immune system.*

Through this process of contamination, your body becomes more susceptible to disease. The glandular centers are not thoroughly stimulated as they need to be. The entire body is somewhat weakened.

Now, if you had a perfect body in which your soul had not chosen a predisposition to certain types of illness or other challenges to the body in this lifetime, then, a long period of sadness without joy would most likely simply result in a feeling of physical weakness, a period of feeling drained, and not being so vital and alive.

But, most ones' souls have chosen *some* tendencies to weaknesses in parts of the body—a certain predisposition to certain illnesses. Thus, the prolonged periods of misery and joylessness might result in confused cellular growth—cancerous growth and other areas—which are directly related to the turbulence in the blood processes caused by protracted sadness and lack of joy.

We are not suggesting that if you have a period of sadness without joy, you will have cancer, or you will fall into terrible disease. But, some of you have a predisposition to those areas, and, if you go *long* periods of time without enough joy, there is more likelihood that you will trigger some of those tendencies to ill health.

But, most ones' souls have chosen *some* tendencies to weaknesses in parts of the body—a certain predisposition to certain illnesses. Thus, the prolonged periods of misery and joylessness might result in confused cellular growth—cancerous growth and other areas—which are directly related to the turbulence in the blood processes caused by protracted sadness and lack of joy.

So, the joy, and the celebration of life, not only make you feel better emotionally, and bring about satisfying and fulfilling inner experiences, but, when easily and naturally cultivated through the years—all other factors being equal—the joy stimulates more strength and health in your physical body.

However, if you ignore your body and treat it

poorly, in terms of the care and feeding of your body, then joy itself may not prevent some debilitation and downturn of health.

If you are intelligent in the care, and feeding, and use of your body, and there is enough joy, then you can expect what you might call the "optimum" health of which your makeup is capable in this lifetime.

Thus, when you set out upon a path in which you intend to celebrate life more, to have more joy in your day-to-day life, then you are moving toward a more satisfying life in all areas of your human expression, mentally, emotionally, and physically.

❖

Question and Answer

NOTE: The following question was asked by a man who is a scientist and is very intellectual. He was struggling with a feeling of resentment against life because he has been so depressed in this lifetime. The Guides' answer to his question sheds light on some of the blockages that people have to attaining joy, particularly too much stress upon the intellect.

QUESTION: I have a general feeling of resentment and anger against life for many years of depression that I have experienced. Because of my various problems over the years, I've generally had the feeling of a constant desperation and unhappiness. Your teachings, and many other teachings, are that our personality is the construction of our soul, and that our life path is part of the soul choices. I feel the anger and resentment that my path is something that I have no choice, or part in, and, therefore, it was imposed upon me by my soul. Do you have any insights that could give me any help in dealing with this persistent resentment and anger?

THE GUIDES: It is important to acknowledge and accept the troubling thoughts and feelings that you are creating in this area. If you attempt to go against them, to force yourself into beliefs that seem untrue to you, then you will continue to torture yourself and feel even more lost than in the past.

Your difficulty in believing areas that do not seem true to you is an important experience that you are having in this lifetime. The fact that you unintentionally prolong your struggle is not something to blame yourself for, but something that you need to be aware of. You can learn, through various mental and emotional adjustments, that you can shorten the time that you spend in misery. By voluntarily focusing upon certain new thoughts and feelings about the truth of life, you can lift yourself from despair and begin to move toward joy. If a certain portion of you cannot actually believe in the underlying truth related to those thoughts and feelings, it does not diminish the effectiveness of their impact upon your mood.

Imagine that you would say that the entire world has been created by a giant cat that is purple. And, each time that you think that, there is a wave of relief and joy. Then, your intellect would come forward and say, "This is absurd. It cannot be true that a giant purple cat has created the world. Therefore, since it is not true, I now deny myself the joy that I attain by pretending that it is true." In other words, you have such a stubborn allegiance to the *intellectual* analysis of life to find truth, which involves refining life to a *factual* basis, that your intellect has become your god. That has temporarily blotted out your intuitive capacity to sense what you might call the *true God*.

Thus, you need to be more and more flexible and creative in allowing yourself to enjoy the benefit of more refined thinking about life. You can even bring forth the flexibility and the willingness to enjoy comforting thoughts about life that may seem *non-logical*. That would be a very large breakthrough for you. For greater joy, you simply need to continue to move in that direction.

At times, you can even pretend that you believe that you have chosen to come into life on earth. No matter how miserable you are, you can pretend that you made a choice. If you do that, you can begin to feel a sense of power.

If you insist upon *logic* in all of your ideas about life, then you will continually diminish the very mental and emotional openings that can bring you comfort and relief, such as temporarily believing in a giant purple cat as the creator of the world. If you are willing to play and experiment with new beliefs, then you will create a temporary halting of the storm of emotional turmoil long enough so that new feelings can begin to take hold—feelings of calm and peace.

Then, occasionally, you can celebrate the joy of

being in a human form without demanding that you have the ultimate intellectual explanation for *why* you are here, and without constantly arguing in your mind about who is responsible for you being here.

All of this is on what you could call the "positive" side.

On the "negative" side, you need to continue to be angry when your angry feelings arise, without being afraid of those feelings. For brief moments, you can freely curse life, and your soul, for placing you in a situation that does not match your ideal.

Part of the challenge with your strong feelings of despair in this lifetime is that you have lived such joyful lives in other lifetimes that, non-consciously, you know that it is possible to have a fully joyful human experience. You can sense the profound joy that you *should* be having, the feelings of goodness that you believe that you *should* be having. So, you might say, "A certain anger is in order. I am angry because this life is not what it should be."

Yet, in the placing of blame upon life for your misery, you are pointing in the wrong direction. The cause of your misery is *your mental and emotional patterns*, as you have responded to your challenges in this lifetime. Thus, you might blame yourself for at times being stubborn, frightened, over-intellectual, resistant to emotional intimacy—all of those areas. When we speak of "blaming" yourself, of course, we are speaking playfully.

When you can see that the causative factors in

your misery are your choices, then choices that seem to you to be imposed upon you by your soul, or fate, or whatever you choose to blame, are not real causes. They arise from stubborn mental and emotional patterns. You can begin to break down the stubborn patterns *emotionally*. Then, your *mind* can follow.

You would need to ask yourself, "How have I made myself miserable by loathing challenging experiences that I have had?" Analyze those thoughts, and emotions, and responses. Even though it is not a joy to grapple with negative situations, you can make adjustments so that it is not so miserable to deal with them. Creating anger and blaming life is an unintentional rationalization for the cause of badness that you feel, and it prevents you from seeing the choices that you make that have made you miserable.

All of this is very difficult to understand when you only use *logic* to search for an ultimate causation of your suffering. But, when you simply live these suggestions day by day, even if at times you believe in a purple cat creating the world, and even if you must occasionally curse life, you can come to see how you make yourself miserable by certain choices. Then, you can make some beneficial adjustments in those choices.

Once there is not your insistence upon ultimate outcome, ultimate defining of causation, ultimate mental explaining of all the factors, then there comes more and more, not so much perfect understanding for your mind, but *comfort* in your pathway. You will be less frightened. You will be less miserable. This does not present *answers*. This does not solve the ultimate riddles of life. But, it brings you the joy that you need.

There will be no perfectly satisfactory *answers* as long as you are in this present personality. But, there can be satisfactory choices that you make, such as the choice to pay more attention to others, to celebrate yourself more fully. Although these will not bring ultimate answers, know that they will bring the comfort that you need.

So, continue to "battle" this area. Question, curse, blame—whatever you wish to do—but always return to the wonderful adjustments that you can make emotionally. In time, when you have enough harmony and joy, and the fear is not so great, you will have more of the deep sensings of the perfect Forces of God. And, in time, you can create with your mind, satisfactory answers to these areas. But, without the comfort, without the deepened intuitive experiences, no intellectual answer can satisfy.

❖

The Guides' Closing Teaching

In this period of human time on earth, the vast numbers of humans who have seen, *vicariously*, the severe challenges that are taking place throughout the physical world—particularly the challenges occurring in your United States—have stimulated a great capacity for *fear*. Yet, most of the humans in your

country are not personally having the severe
challenges that are brought to your attention by your
communication channels. They have not been
personally attacked by violent groups of individuals,
they have not been poisoned by unusual germs, they
are not destitute and living in the streets. For most of
them, all of the areas of the outer world that they fear
are in their thoughts and emotions, although a few
are certainly suffering in physical ways.

In this period, the primary challenge for you
ones is not the negative events in the physical world.
It is your *fear*. And, as many of you are beginning to
realize, the primary challenge in life has always been
your fear, and always will be, until the fear is healed.

So, each day, say to yourself:

> **"My joy does not depend upon there being a
> perfect world where there is no violence, no
> poverty, no illness, no hunger. My joy depends
> upon my *response* to the world as it exists in this
> day, even some areas that do not please me. My
> joy depends upon *me*—how I work with my
> thoughts, and feelings, and responses to life in
> the world around me."**

When you realize the truth of this, then, most of
your attention will go to *you*—your thoughts, and
feelings, and responses—not to a constant focus on
the challenges in the world.

❖

Then, you could say, "My joy also depends upon my
relationships with other humans. If I have no

relationships, it diminishes my joy. If I have painful ones, it brings a bit of joy, a bit of pain. If I have deeply loving relationships, it brings great joy."

So, the *inner adjustments* that you make in your own patterns, and the *outer expressions* with other humans, are the two legs upon which you walk your human pathway. If one leg is weak, you limp and it is more painful. If both legs are strong, you dance through life.

You can remember this by saying to yourself:

"In strengthening both legs, I will be loving, patient, and kind with myself. I will notice the choices that I make that bring me pain, and I will make some adjustments in them. As I heal them I will have more joy. The other leg is my relationships with the humans around me. If those relationships are not satisfying enough, I will make some changes to them. If they are satisfying, I will build upon that. If I have no meaningful relationships, I will achieve some."

We are not saying that you could not be happy alone. You could be. But, your experience of life is not likely to be as deep and as satisfying as it can be if you feel that you are appreciated and loved by other humans, and, that you appreciate and love other humans yourself.

So, when you need a simple guideline to urge you forward to more joy, look at those two areas: (1) the awakening of your choices, the enlivening and enlightenment of your choices; and (2) the deepening of your relationships with other humans.

Then, if you would think in terms of adding to those two, *an experience of the Divine*, then, you would truly master this human world.

❖

For the moment, as we pour forth our love into your heart, make a gentle feeling that would say:

> "When I am focusing upon my inner awakening and enlightenment, and when I am focusing upon the love of other humans, and when I am focusing upon the Divine, then I am doing what I need to do for the greatest joy and fulfillment in this lifetime."

The rest is a matter of *refinement*—doing all of it more wonderfully, more sensitively—as you move forward in the remaining years that you have left in your present body.

For this moment, without concern for the many complexities of joy and love that we have been exploring with you, say to yourself:

> "Each day, I will celebrate *me*, and I will celebrate my choices, and I will continue to build upon my choices in more wonderful ways in the future. So, I expect more joy, and I expect more love in the future of this lifetime."

As we love you and guide you, use the power of God Itself that lives within you to create the potent thoughts and feelings that say:

> "I am doing so well as me, and I will expect more joy and love in the remaining years of this lifetime."

Think that, and feel that in this moment. Then, as you go forth into your daily affairs and *live* that, day by day, you will truly draw upon the healing power of joy to bring the great fulfillment that you desire in this lifetime.

And, for this time in earth, the speaking is ended.

❖ ❖ ❖

CHAPTER 4

The Fourth Reading

The Guides' Opening Teaching

We would suggest now, as an adjustment within the human *self*, a certain "paralleling" of your life in your imagination as an "experimental model," you might say.

Often, as you ones live your lives, it is as though you are a gambling one and you constantly fear the loss of your money. So, if you practice gambling *without* money, then you can feel that you can learn without so much fear of loss. Thus, it is very wise to have a kind of occasional practice of "parallel living" in your mind.

Most ones tend to do this naturally as you try out various ideas and approaches to life. But, if you do it as a formal process, you can begin, as the gambling one without money at risk, to view your imaginary life *without fear* in order to analyze the flaws in your strategy that would lead to loss. Then, you can adjust those and move toward gain.

In this parallel experiencing, or *life-creation*, you would recognize the aspects of your choices that diminish the power of joy in your life. You would recognize patterns of lack of patience, certain stubbornness areas, certain areas that are familiar and comfortable but usually darken your pathway and lead to sadness, and pain, and separation. You would calmly assess the many areas of your inner life that make it difficult for you to have full joy.

❖

This assessment process can be done briefly each day for a few moments, usually in the morning before you enter into the complexities of your daily life in the physical world.

You would begin the process by imagining how you will live out the coming day, according to the tasks that you will accomplish in that day. You would say, "Today I will work in this way, with these persons, doing this task, with these results." In your imagining, you will proceed to live those experiences as you always have with your usual thoughts, feelings, attitudes, and choices about how to behave. But, in this process, instead of actually living out the choices and being totally caught up in them, you "preview" them from "outside" of the experiences in a calm, objective way that is not dominated by your past experience and past habits.

Let us say that you work in the office of a large business. Each day, you go forward into your work and there is a supervising one above you who, it appears, is not fond of you. So, each day, you have a feeling of not being appreciated, even a sense of being criticized, although you are never verbally criticized by the one. From that experience with the supervising one, you have a feeling of displeasure, a certain sadness, a frustration in the work, and you feel bad during your working day.

Now, in your "previewing" process of imagining in the morning, as you imagine going forward in your working arena, you first re-create in your imagination the usual experience of feeling criticized, unappreciated, and being sad and miserable throughout the day. As you do that, it should become clear to you that *you* are actually *creating* your negative feelings out of habit because your supervising one is not there with you causing you to have those negative feelings in that moment. You can realize that your creation of your negative feelings is the real challenge, not your supervisor. You can realize that many humans are unappreciated by supervisors, but they do not create constant negative feelings and live miserable days in the working arena. They have different responses from yours.

So, in your previewing process, you begin to experiment in your imagination with *new* responses. And, all of this is done quite briefly and easily. You imagine yourself not having the same responses of negativity that you have had in the past. You might imagine that the supervising one does not even approach you in that day. You can imagine many other ways to feel joyful about the coming day.

The same could be done if you are planning to visit a friend and you wish to have some joy in the visit, but you have had some challenge with the friend in the past. You preview the visit in order to identify beforehand what choices will generally produce what results, without having to live through them again and again out of habit, or out of the pressure of the situation.

If you are prepared beforehand with a bit of creative imagining about the coming events of each day, and you have some new ideas in mind for responding in new ways, then, even under a bit of pressure of old habits, it is simpler to actually carry out your new ideas. This simple focal point, practiced daily, will enhance the joy that you have in all situations. It will show you the great potency and power that you have to *create* joy, instead of waiting for joy to fall upon you by good fortune.

❖

In many areas of life, you ones need to make a clear distinction in your own mind between *joy* and *bliss*. Most of you have had certain human experiences in past lifetimes of a rather strong engagement with the Divine. In that, you have experienced *pure bliss*. You have reveled in it, you have pursued it, hungered for more of it. In this lifetime, for those of you with a great passion for the experience of the Divine, because of your hunger for that kind of *bliss*, even when you make great *joy* in certain moments, the joy can seem not strong enough.

This is as though you are used to eating in the finest restaurants as a wealthy one. Then, you become poor and you go to the meanest places to eat. Even though it is nourishing food, it always seems not good enough. It is always lacking something.

Many of you ones have had quite a bit of joy in this lifetime, but, it never seems deep enough. What you are hungry for is *bliss*.

A few of you have had the wonderful experience of bliss in *this* lifetime, and it tends to overshadow the simple joys of your daily life. You can now understand that you must *re-train* yourself to appreciate the simple joys when you cannot attain bliss. Joy is not a substitute for bliss, for you will always desire bliss, and long for it, and try to achieve it as often as you can. But, at times, you must be satisfied with, and fully appreciate, and deeply *feel*, the "lesser," but nourishing fare of the "poor" restaurant of human joy experience. Then, occasionally, you will have some inner wealth and you will go to the finer restaurant of the Divine and experience some bliss. In this *integration of joy and bliss*, you have a beneficial pattern for your entire life.

Most of you ones have such strong *desires* and *ambitions* that you will always long for something quite extraordinary, whether it is joy, love, attainment, health, sexual pleasure, creative expression, whatever it might be. If you do not train yourself to appreciate the "smaller" experiences of achievement, then you will become quite discontent under your passion for the perfect and totally fulfilling experience.

Work patiently in this area. You will always continue to strive for the more intense experiences of goodness, but, you can learn to celebrate and rejoice in that which seems more ordinary to you. If you are a starving person, you can rejoice in a crust of bread. If you have great wealth, you can rejoice in a grand feast. Emotionally, at times, you are starving, and, at other times, you are wealthy. You can learn to celebrate both as part of the extraordinary human experience that you are creating in this lifetime.

❖

When you ones came into this lifetime, your soul established certain "directions" for your human *self*. This is similar to having plans and instructions for a child that you have. You can send your child forth to the marketplace with instructions to buy certain foods with a certain amount of money. If the child returns with exactly what you have requested, you rejoice. If the child makes some changes in the request, purchases items that you are not fond of, perhaps you do not rejoice as much, but, *you do not condemn the child*, for you wish the child to grow strong in its confidence and its decision making.

When you came into this earth, your human *self* had certain strong intentions that *you-as-a-soul* placed into you for many important purposes, many reasons, many accomplishments in many different areas of life. Since we are looking at the area of joy, you could say that your soul has placed into you certain *intentions* to create joy *in certain ways.* These would be the "instructions" given to you to go to the market and purchase the *perfect* foods, as seen by your soul with its higher wisdom.

Your soul, as the "parent," would say to you-the-child, "Bring vegetables and the nourishing fruits." But, at times, you-the-child will return with the candies. This is not bad. *You-as-the-soul* do not condemn you-the-child. But, you hope that the child will bring the nourishing foods the next time. The candy is sweet, but not so nourishing.

Certain pleasures that you ones have sought out for joy in this lifetime are sweet, but they are not so nourishing. The experiences are strong and intense when you have them, but, the experience of joy can fade away fast. And, at times, those pleasures can leave you feeling empty and undernourished within. You each can recognize these kinds of choices in your own life.

Know that, within you, there is a strong impulse, or tendency, placed into you by your soul, to buy the nourishing food. Your soul nudges you toward the human experiences that are deeply joyful and meaningful at the same time.

For each of you, these soul impulses would vary slightly, for you each have had some different lifetimes in which you learned to rejoice in life in slightly different ways. For example, imagine that in your past lifetime, you enjoyed a slow, leisurely lifetime as the owner of a tavern. In that lifetime, joy for you was pleasant social interactions and profit monetarily. Thus, your soul would give you a tendency to enjoy that kind of experience in this lifetime.

However, in this lifetime, if you do not choose to own a tavern and create joy in that same way, your soul will not say, "I now condemn you and reject you." Your soul rejoices in the choices that you make in how you wish to attain joy in this lifetime.

We are attempting to show you that there is always a capacity for *new* joy in you. Your soul has given you many more impulses toward joy than you could possibly follow in one lifetime.

Some of your present choices may follow some of those soul impulses. Usually, you can feel those areas. They are deeper in joy, and more steady. They are the nourishing food from the marketplace. They are less likely to disappoint you than some others that are the candies from the market.

Know that you have these deep soul impulses. Yet, know that your soul will not force them upon you. Your soul will not choose for you. *You* must decide how you will create joy in this lifetime.

❖

If you notice that your joy areas seem a bit thin, not so nourishing, and you fret that perhaps you will never know the truly nourishing joy, be assured that you have the soul impulses within you to move toward the fuller joy. You have simply not yet become aware of them and followed them thoroughly enough.

So, if you are in a position where mostly your joys are infrequent and rather small—they are not that intense—and there is a kind of flatness, or ennui, in your feelings most of the time, and there is a sense of having depleted possibilities, or the sense that there is no possible joyful expression for you, know that this is *a temporary confusion.* For your soul has more than filled you with certain impulses that could attract you to an activity, or a person, or a grouping, or an experience, that could be more joyful in a meaningful, nourishing way. Simply know that such impulses exist within you. You need only awaken to them, invite them forward and experiment with them.

❖

Now, many humans will need a *pattern* to follow toward greater joy. They cannot believe that they have enough wisdom on their own to set out on an original path of joy. So, usually, they look for a path that is already open or identified by other persons. That can be beneficial for some.

If you have a friend who excels in the stock-marketing, and has wealth, freedom, and a sense of excitement and adventure, and you are feeling quite flat and mostly joyless in your life, you might say, "I wish to do the stock-marketing." If you actually have a talent for that, and a fascination with it, then it might be your path of deeper joy.

So, it is certainly not wrong to follow others, particularly if you have tried to open your own passion, creativity, and interest, and you appear to be failing. Then, you might use others as examples, picking out the most fascinating ones that you know of, and perhaps trying to emulate their choices of activity, behavior, attitude, occupation—whatever you find inspiring about them.

Most of you would benefit from following the *positive* patterns of sensitive, loving individuals. As you set out upon a pathway similar to theirs, you might find that it is the path with the deepest joy for you.

❖

Another way to create a path toward joy in life is to follow your own thoughts and feelings. You might instinctively know that certain ways of pursuing life bring deeper joy. Or, you might find your way through "trial and error," experimenting with different ways of creating joy and noticing which paths bring less joy—even some pain and misery—and which paths bring you the deeper joy in life.

The self-choosing of the pathway is the way that humans are *intended* to learn and grow, which might involve some challenge. You ones were not intended to come into this earth and be given the perfect father and mother, with perfect patterns, in which every moment is joyful and uneventful, in terms of challenge and learning.

This is as though you are sent into the jungle to hunt the game to feed your tribe. When there comes difficulty, if you run away, you will never feed the tribe. They will go hungry. If you stand fast and overcome the difficulty, you will become an expert hunter and the tribe will feast.

In a very *crude* way of speaking, you are "feeding" your soul. Your soul has desired a journey through the jungle of human life, and has come forth as *you.* If you retreat from the complexity, your soul has very meager learning, and fulfillment, and expansion. If you engage your life intensely, then your soul, which is *you,* has a great expansion, and the wonderful fulfillment of the purposes for coming into human form.

Your soul does not say that you *must* follow the path of full engagement with all of the experiences of your life in order to master. But, it should be quite clear, from the repetitive experiences that constantly arise in your life, from the consistent desires and interests that you have, that the greater fulfillment is achieved by living all of that fully, since it keeps on presenting itself to you through the years. You should know yourself well enough at this point in your life to know that your repetitive patterns, interests, desires, challenges, confusions, are all part of mastering the jungle of human life on earth.

❖

Now, your soul has intended for your human life to be a *joyful* mastering, not a frightening one. Fear is human-created. Fear is the "dross" of confused human choices.

Your soul *could* bring you forth ignoring the negative patterns from your past lifetimes of earth. In a way that is difficult for the human mind to understand, that would add a darkness and heaviness to the lives of all other humans.

By your soul choosing to take up in your present human *self*, certain tendencies that are confused, various challenging patterns—which at times can seem to diminish your joy—that opens the way for your mastery, and your mastery becomes a certain *miraculous upliftment* for all of humanity. This is an area that you ones may never see, or be able to fully understand. Simply know that you as a human *self* are doing your part in carrying and transforming the burden for humanity, instead of shifting it to others by insisting upon a life that is totally free from challenge.

Even though the hidden complexities of this would be very difficult for you ones to understand, simply thinking about your personal mastery as a contribution to humanity can help you be more patient with the periods in which you are not achieving enough joy, and in which there are so many complexities that seem to be a nuisance, or a threat, or too much of a burden for you personally.

❖

When we point to challenge tendencies given to you by your soul to master, we are not speaking of your *personal fears* that you create. If each day, over a long period of time, you have a vague sense of, "I will never be loved in this lifetime," then, most likely, that is a pattern from a past lifetime that *you-as-a-soul* have chosen for you to master in this lifetime. But, if you constantly *fear* that you will never be loved, and that fear goes on for many years and you never heal it by creating love in your life, then that was not intended by your soul. You are unintentionally prolonging a fear by your own confusion, or inertia, or passiveness, or inactivity, or unwillingness to fully engage the pattern of fear and master it.

So, you ones have a very ambiguous kind of path here. On the one hand, you come forth from your soul with a primary intention of joy, fulfillment, and love in the human world, and your soul gives you *many* talents and abilities to achieve that. On the other hand, for many important but complex reasons, your soul has given you a *few* threads of challenge patterns to master. Thus, you have taken upon yourself, if you will, the "cross" of various challenges, a kind of "sacrifice," but one that is extremely important. Therefore, your human path is not intentionally free of challenge. It is not intentionally continual happiness, harmony. But, certainly, it is not intentionally constant misery. That is the human creation part that arises from fear.

If you ones did not *create fear* about challenges, then you would have occasional fussing, fretting, tension, doubt, stress, and pain, but rarely would you have strong fear in life. And, rarely would you have self-diminishment thoughts and feelings.

This is a very delicate area. You ones must accept a certain burden of challenge in human life, but, you need not tolerate excessive self-created burden. That is the area that can so easily cloud your joy, and darken your path, until you learn how you create your excessive fears and emotional negativity. Once you understand how you create that subjective negativity, then you can draw upon your inner power to release the old patterns and create the new patterns of great joy in your life.

So, if you ones have the intention, the will, the stamina, the determination, you can live a life relatively free of strong fear, panic, terror, despair . You will have mostly joy and harmony, with occasional stress, doubt, sadness—the less intense experiences of negativity.

If your burdens seem too heavy and dark, then you need to continue to identify the confused thoughts and emotions that have exaggerated your inner negativity. You need to discover the inner strength and creativity that your soul has given you so that you can create the full joy that *you-as-a-soul* intended for your present human *self* in this lifetime.

❖

Questions and Answers

Note: In the following question, a woman asks about an experience of release of negativity that she had during the

Retreat. The Guides' answer shows how releasing various restricting mental and emotional patterns can open the way for tapping in to the power of joy. The answer also stresses the importance of people extending Divine Love into the human world, and gives a deep metaphysical viewpoint on *perfection*.

QUESTION ONE: I went for a walk at lunchtime and I knew there was something that needed to be released. I let a lot of sadness come up. It felt like the joy was just buried in the sadness. It felt very, very good to release the sadness. I wonder if you could comment on this experience of release that I had?

THE GUIDES: Looking at the various patterns within you, there stands out a certain *reluctance to trust earth life*. This relates to your desire for goodness, and perfection, and efficiency in the earth world that can cause you to feel that *you* must create the goodness or there will be none. Your desire for goodness is quite beneficial in your daily life in the family, in teaching, and in helping others, but, at times, this tends to spill over into a kind of over-perfecting of yourself, which can at times becomes limiting.

This is as though you are working in the fields drawing forth the cottons from the plants. You earn a great deal of money doing this work. When it is time to rest, out of habit, you continue to work in the fields because you are afraid you do not have enough money. Here, you need to learn that you do not always need to work. You need to learn a certain playfulness, and less seriousness toward yourself. This requires a trust that you are not such a terrible person that you need to constantly perfect yourself. Perhaps you can actually, at times, stop trying to become better and simply enjoy how far you have come in this lifetime.

At times, this is simply a matter of surrendering to who you are, trusting that you are good enough, and you do not need to try to be more perfect. Then, at other times, it is a kind of surrender to God, or to the Divine. You simply trust that you are deeply loved by Divine Beings, and the moment is good enough without trying to be more loved.

There are different variations in terms of what you might be thinking or feeling in the moment, but, in these areas that you are speaking of, the sense of *release* is the key. Not only to release to a feeling of being wonderful in the moment, but also stirring up a kind of joy that does not need to be manufactured, or pursued.

We have spoken of ways to use your power of thought and emotion to choose to *create* joyful experiences. But, in the experience of release that you had, there is a different kind of joy that you are working with, a joy in which you cease to *do* at all. In your releasing, the beauty of nature so soothed you and penetrated you that you could feel the joy, and, your orientation toward the Divine prompted you to awaken certain inner sensings so that you could begin to feel loved without doing anything. You began to feel goodness without trying to *create* the goodness yourself. You gave in to it. *You celebrated goodness without pushing and forcing toward it.* This is a very important way of experiencing joy that all ones can begin to learn.

You can experience the Divine and have it remain a personal experience within your human *self.* In the past, that would have been enough for you. You would not have felt a need to pour that forth into the human realm. Now, in the broadest, deepest sense, you are moving along a "continuum of perfection" to extend Divine Perfection into human experience.

In other words, to clarify, at the "purest" end of the spectrum of Divine Perfection is the *unmanifested* Force of Life that you would call God— pure in its perfection and in its self-containedness.

Then, there comes the "movement" of this God Force along the spectrum of Divine Perfection into *the manifestation of realms.*

Then, there eventually comes the manifestation of Divine Perfection in the human expression in its *true* potential in the beginning of life on earth, without the interference of human confusion.

This long continuum of Divine Perfection is then *extended by human choice into physical matter.* This is where the perfection becomes less perfect, due to the confused human choices through the ages. Thus, this is where there comes to be the need for humans who are willing to extend Divine Perfection into present human life on earth in order to transform the human negativity that has obscured the pure perfection of the Divine on earth.

In certain past lifetimes, you have been content with allowing the joy and harmony of Divine Perfection to "stop" at your own personal experience, keeping it "inside," so to speak. So, the continuum was cut off at your personal point.

Then, in certain later lifetimes, you did awaken to the fact that *you-as-a-human* are the Creator *in the physical world*, and thus, you are an extension of the God Force coming forth from *the eternal world*. As Divine Perfection comes into your human *self*, you can either *stop* the continuum of perfection within you, or, you can *extend* it outward through your personal choice of kindness, compassion, and love expressed in the human world.

This is quite a profound area for all humans. You have had some important, meaningful experiences that hint at, or point toward, a great mystery of human life. That mystery can be stated in this way:

> **If humans do not choose to extend the Divine Perfection, then it will not be extended out into the human world in tangible ways, but will remain beneath human conscious awareness. The human world then turns to challenge, pain, suffering, and chaos. And, that is as it will be** *until human choices are changed.*

When you go forth in this lifetime making various inner adjustments to align yourself with the Divine, and then you choose to share Divine Love in your own way with other humans, you are personally extending the Divine Perfection into the human world in wonderful and important ways.

❖

NOTE: This question was asked by a woman who was feeling flat in her meditation practice. She felt that this was related to a lack of joy in daily life. In the Guides' answer to her question, there are very helpful suggestions for anyone dealing with such experiences.

QUESTION TWO: For about the past year or so, my spiritual attunements have been sort of dry, in the sense of rarely getting that deeply felt sense of connection with the Divine that I used to get on a more regular basis. I've continued to attune on pretty much a daily basis, but it has been a long period of time, waiting for something to kick back in. The conditions of my life in general feel fairly settled and happy. I feel like I've accomplished a lot in many areas, but I find that there's just not much of a sense of excitement or passion right now in what I'm doing. Is there something that I'm doing that's blocking my joy and passion in life? Are there some patterns that I need to look at? And, if so, do you have some specific suggestions for me about that?

THE GUIDES: This is a very delicate area, for it is wise to allow such feelings to nag at you for a while. To frantically rush at them to find a solution and make dramatic changes might cause confusion in the future.

For example, imagine that you are bored with your mating one. Instead of simply experiencing the feelings of boredom and sorting through various choices that have brought about that experience, you rush out to find a new mating one. That would not be wrong, or bad, but, for this lifetime, you would have lost the opportunity to penetrate the fascinating complexities and mystery of your present mating one—to discover many areas that can be quite beneficial for you to know about yourself, and about your interaction with loved ones.

In responding to a lack of joy at this time, your tendency would be to say, "Since I am not so joyful about my present life activities and attunements, that means that there is something wrong. I must find out what that is so that I can *eliminate* it so that the joy can return."

This is a very delicate area to speak to you about because it is not *wrong* for you to rush at this area to find causes and try to eliminate them. You have the right to do that. It is not wrong to even begin new activities to re-stimulate joy. But, for the present, if it pleases you, we gently suggest that you refrain from doing that. We ask that you would be willing to *fully experience* the feelings of flatness, or sameness, so that before you *change* them, you can *learn* from them.

There are different ways to look at this area of lack of joy that will lead you to different conclusions about what the patterns are. We cannot choose for you which way to look at this area. But, we can suggest four potential perspectives. You can decide which one pleases you, and you can work with that for a while.

You are so *intense*, intellectually and emotionally, and you have such a passion for intensity that, after certain ongoing experiences of marriage, childbirth, child loving, teaching, serving, helping others heal—all of which are quite wonderful in many ways—with the *repetition* of those experiences, the feeling of *intensity* has decreased. Thus, the first suggested way of viewing this is to say to yourself, "As a passionate person, I am passing through the natural human process of growing discontent with what I continually repeat. I grow used to familiar experiences, thus, I fail to fully appreciate them. As a consequence, I am not fully investing my intensity into those familiar areas. I am not urging myself to have more intensity. I am allowing a natural human tendency toward repetitive experience becoming dull to dominate my life. Therefore, I need to *create* new joyful ways to inwardly experience my attunement, my family, my work, myself."

This might be the most difficult approach, for you would be pulling yourself up by your own feet, so to speak. You would be *creating your own inner joy*, rather than rushing around to find new experiences in the physical world that would automatically make you feel the joy. Yet, this approach would be the most stimulating one, for, once you achieve the *rejuvenation* of your own inner experience through your own creativity without relying upon outer circumstances to do it for you, then you would know that you are truly a powerful human being *who can create joy in life no matter what your emotions are doing.*

The second viewpoint is to say to yourself, "I need more stimulating experiences in the outer world. I am tired of some of the old ones that I have. Instead of working with my mental and emotional patterns to create new joy in the old areas, I will seek out new experiences that will bring me joy." Now, this approach is not wrong. It is not less good than the first area. It is simply not as masterful. But, certainly, you are not prohibited from making this choice, and if you make this choice you do not suddenly become a bad person. Your soul will continue to fully love you.

You might choose to do a mixture of the first two approaches. You might seek out some new friends, some new activities that are different, that cause you to feel, "Now, it is easier to be stimulated in joy." In the second area, the activities stimulate you. In the first area, you stimulate yourself, whether your activities change or not. You could choose to "mix" the two areas.

The third viewpoint is to take an entirely differ-ent perspective on *yourself.* You can say to yourself, playfully, "I have had enough addiction to *intensity.* It is time to find joy in a mature, more steady, more peaceful, less exciting expression." This is also very difficult to accomplish, but it has a kind of "eternal" quality to it.

It is quite difficult to put this eternal quality into words. We would need to say that, in the *soul* experience, there is no "excitement." Instead, there is Divine Bliss, and a total completion in love.

Crudely speaking, we would say that the souls' "desire" for "excitement" is a desire for a certain kind of *intensity* that can be gained in the physical world. That is the reason that souls send forth human *selfs* into the physical world.

When humans have had *enough* of intensity, which generally occurs naturally as you ones age and mature, there can come a choice of adopting this third viewpoint, which can be seen as, "riding the experience of maturity," which is calmer, less exciting, less stimulating, but often, more deeply fulfilling. And, if seen appropriately, it is more Divine, more eternal. The difficulty in showing you this is that the human words do not truly reveal these wonderful truths and the powerful joy that this level of experience offers. So, you must take the words deeper in your own mind and feelings in order to know the truth that we are trying to show you here.

The fourth viewpoint is to give up responsibility and focus only upon yourself, which can be quite exciting. You can focus upon your sexual pleasure, your intellectual curiosity, pleasures of the world, of the body. You can move about at your own will. You can become more self-involved. You could be very stimulated by this for a brief period. Then, your maturity and your idealism would return and you would say, "Perhaps this is not the way to achieve the intensity of joy that I desire." Yet, to be truly free, you must know that you have the freedom to make this choice if you desire it. Your soul will not suddenly say that you are a bad person.

The key here is to know that there is nothing *wrong* with your present experience of lack of joy, except that the experience is not as pleasing as you wish it to be, particularly in the attunement area. Since you have certain *expectations* of a more joyful and inspiring attunement, then you notice rather consistently that your attunement experience is *not* that. Thus, there is a kind of inner "rejection" of the un-joyful experience, and that actually *blocks* the possibility of having a deeper experience.

If you can rejoice in a moderate attunement experience, or even a feeling that there is no attunement at all, you will break through to the truth that you are *always* being fed by Divine Love. The only thing that fluctuates is *your conscious awareness* of that love.

In this area, you can feel more love and joy by not *trying* to feel more love and joy. You can appreciate the fact that you have the freedom to make an attunement, even a one that seems not so interesting. You can appreciate the fact that you can breathe, and be alive, while you are attuning. You can appreciate the fact that you are not filled with cancerous growth in the body. That you are not living in poverty and squalor, pain and suffering.

So, here, it is simply a matter of *appreciation*, and the very calm acceptance of the moment, even when your inner experience does not please you. Be patient with the *un-joy* period. We suggest that you do not rush to change it, but perhaps you experiment with some of these viewpoints in a playful manner, knowing that there is nothing wrong with your present experience, and, there is certainly nothing wrong with *you* as a wonderful human *self* who is having the present experience of un-joy.

❖

NOTE: A strong influence upon the amount of joy a person feels is their physical environment. In the following question, a woman in the group asks about the way that people respond to their physical location. The answer reveals that some of the factors are related to past lifetimes. A portion of her answer is given here.

QUESTION THREE: I have noticed that for myself and others, physical location seems to influence the feelings of joy. Some people love the ocean or the mountains. I love lakes and woods. I also have found a strong negative reaction to the desert. The heat, the desolation and the openness of it, often have felt oppressive. Would you explain why the sense of place should have this kind of an influence on the feelings of joy? And, in particular, why do I have such a negative reaction to the desert, and what can I do to transform those negative feelings into feelings that are more joyful?

THE GUIDES: This can be an important area for the understanding of the human personality *self*. But, usually, the *causes* of such repulsion or attraction to physical places are hidden, for they live in past experiences before the present lifetime.

As a general guideline for yourself, you can say to yourself, "When I have rather *consistent* strong likes and dislikes, in terms of place, unless I am quite aware of experiences from this life that explain those strong likes and dislikes, then I can rest assured that I am working with extremely strong patterns from past lifetimes of earth." And, you can sense some of that here with the desert areas, even though your conscious awareness of the past lifetime experiences is not fully present.

Looking first of all at the watery, wooded areas, there are a number of lifetimes in those kinds of places in which the joy of your earth life emanated primarily from the *romantic love* area. In many of those lifetimes, love was associated with a certain wealth, creativity, and, what you might call culture, refinement, extraordinary sensitivity to physical beauty in all areas—the artistic beauty, the many wonderful areas of nature beauty. In some of the lifetimes, particularly in a portion of the Switzerland, there was this extraordinary joy in the love area associated with wealth. These areas are very strong intuitions, strong attractions. It is wise to indulge them as much as practically possible in the present.

NOTE: The above past-life example was one of many given to this woman by the Guides. The rest of her answer was quite personal and is omitted here. The cause of her aversion to desert areas was explained in a detailed account of a very traumatic lifetime in Northern Africa in the distant past.

❖

The Guides' Closing Teaching

Looking now at the unfolding patterns within each of you, there comes a striking similarity in the way in which you ones *internalize knowledge*. That is to say that you ones quickly "swallow" knowledge whole, and then you try to digest it later.

This might be a beneficial way for a *whale* to eat food, but not for a human trying to assess knowledge. So, in taking in our speakings, you need not feel that you must instantly digest and understand everything. You can enjoy the celebration of the human moment, knowing that the "absorption" of knowledge will occur later as you work patiently with these speakings.

This can help you feel that you are not a one who must frantically prepare for a test in the schooling areas, but you are a one simply exploring, at your leisure, the wonderful experience of being human. You can take certain suggestions and directions that we offer at your own pace, in your own time. This is the joyful way to proceed, to celebrate the moment for what it is, to digest knowledge later and add what pleases you.

Each day, you can take such an attitude. You can say to yourself, "I love to learn and grow, but, in this day, my first priority is *to celebrate being alive in human form.* Then, I will make my growing and learning at my own pace and not try to swallow it whole in one day, or in one bite."

When you bring forth this attitude, it affirms to

yourself that you are not frightened of lacking knowledge. If you would say, "I *must* learn *immediately*," and you frantically try to learn, it means that you are discontent with your present *self*, and you are frightened that there is something wrong with being "un-knowledgeable." So, the frantic consumption of knowledge is usually rooted in fear.

The leisurely "nibbling away" at knowledge, at your own pace, is rooted in a trust that there is nothing wrong with *you* in the present. There is nothing wrong with you in the moment that you lack certain knowledge. You can understand that it is wonderful to gain knowledge, but, you do not suddenly become more perfect when you do that. You simply feel more satisfied when you appreciate and gain more knowledge.

So, be leisurely in these areas that we have shown you in these speakings. They are quite important, but, you have much time to explore them, work with them, and add them to your knowledge "repertoire."

❖

For this moment, let yourself feel, "I have absorbed enough knowledge for the moment. Now, I wish to sit quietly to savor, and digest."

So, there comes now a certain feeling of release, relaxation, a feeling that there are no duties in this moment. There is nothing to work at, or strive for. It is as though you are a beautiful deer in the forest, and you have had your fill of the delicious foods. Now, you simply sit in the sun, rejoicing in being alive.

In this moment, as you sit in the sun of Divine Love that is pouring into you, release all that might distract you from that love. Bask in the glow and the warmth of the love. Know that *this moment is precious.* Not a future one in which your life is different, but, *this moment.*

If you cannot feel the preciousness of this moment, then you will have difficulty feeling the preciousness of the next moment, and the next, and the next. So, begin *now.* Stop the rush through life. Stand still in the light of Divine Love. Let it touch you, and rejoice in it now.

And, for this time in earth, the speaking is ended.

❖ ❖ ❖

CHAPTER 5

The Fifth Reading

The Guides' Opening Teaching

We would turn your attention now to the human experience of *time*. The primary challenge here is that you ones have the underlying, *non-conscious* sensing that the experience within time is a temporary illusion, yet, at the *conscious* human level there is the total conviction that time is a reality. As humans, you ones must live through time. You must go from young to old. This push and pull between *truth* and *illusion* often makes a great constraint in the free-flowingness of your joy.

It is as though you are a brilliant singer and you have tied a scarf about your neck to be beautiful in appearance. But, you have made the scarf so tight that there is not the full flowing of your voice, so your performance is diminished.

The constraint of the human illusion of time can squeeze the free-flowingness of your inner *self* so that you are not performing at your highest level of joy or creativity as a human. Yet, if you ignore time and pretend that it is not real, then you can become quite confused and disoriented in the human world. If you are playing a game and you ignore the rules, then you will not have a joyful game.

So, the challenge is the interplay between, on the one hand, a deep but vague sensing that there is something so magnificent that is just out of your grasp—which, of course, is your eternal existence *beyond* time—and, on the other hand, the very clear and "true" sensation from the human point of view that there certainly is time. You ones clearly live within time, moving from one moment to the next, from one year to the next, from youth to maturity.

❖

All of this is usually ignored by most humans. They simply live out their days accepting the powerful "reality" of time. And, the *conscious* joy that you ones achieve clearly occurs within time. But, within time, as you have experienced, your joy *fluctuates*.

Beyond time, in the *eternal*, the joy *never wavers*. The perfection, the love, the harmony, the beauty, the depth of purpose and meaning, the sense of fullness—all of those areas continually exist.

In the human expression within time, the fluctu-ation of joy experiences is lived out quite naturally without much thought given to the hidden realities beneath your conscious awareness. But, for your understanding of the creation of joy and the ways that joy uplifts the human *self*, there can be some benefit in at least considering intellectually the deeper truths that are hidden from your human conscious awareness. However, you would not wish your intellectualizing about this area to interfere with your natural interplay with the physical world within time and space. But, simply having a small grasp of some of the realities that are *not temporary*, that are *eternal*, and occasionally thinking about these areas through your day, can somewhat "jolt" the stubborn patterns of your human *self*, and can break apart some rigidities, and can begin to launch you into a new experience of *timeless joy*.

❖

The first step in moving toward an understanding of timeless joy, and occasionally feeling it, is to learn to observe, in each *present* moment within time, how much you are thinking about *other* moments beyond the present.

Imagine that you are engaged in a very satisfying romantic-sexual encounter with a beloved one. Then, as you are enjoying the pleasure and the love, you begin to think about the *next* time that you will make love with this one in the future. You begin to think about how you will improve that future experience.

After you have done that for a while, you suddenly notice that the love encounter in the present is over. Then, you realize that most of the joy was deflected because your attention was directed beyond the joyful experience in the present moment.

If you have a habit of thinking beyond the

present moment, even *positive* thinking—imagining, planning, speculating—and you find that in moments that usually would be very joyful and quite satisfying, much of your thought attention is directed toward your planning for the future, or ruminating about the past, then you will find the experience of joy to be feeble, or not present at all. So, to have the fuller joy requires a willingness to train your attention upon the experience of the present moment. Most human ones have some difficulty in that, particularly those with active minds.

So, you might say, "One aspect of having more joy in my life, and blessing my human *self* more with that joy, is to take note of the way that I engage the present moment. Do I engage it by thinking about a past or future moment, or, do I pay attention to the present moment as I am living it? Do I let the moment sink in, fully saturate me?"

This is particularly important in achieving joy in your relationships with other humans when you are communicating with them. You need to notice if your attention is directed *beyond* that person, whether it is to your own thoughts, or to thoughts of past or future, or plans, or many areas that are not important in the present moment, but are simply a habit that you create. If you notice that, you might wish to make some adjustments. You might wish to train yourself to notice the other person in each present moment as closely as you can.

❖

When you fully invest yourself in a present moment without rushing to the future or thinking about the past, there comes a new, delicious experience of *intensity*. And, as you practice this for a while, there comes to be a sense of great *importance* about the moment that you are in. When you do not practice this, then most moments do not seem that important.

Imagine that you have a business meeting and your entire career depends upon that meeting. If you are successful, you will have a wealthy position. If you fail to impress ones at the meeting, you will be moved backwards financially.

Thus, you have a great preoccupation with that meeting for three weeks. You are planning, you are fretting, fussing, trying to stimulate confidence. And, during those three weeks, rarely do you live the present moment. You "displace" yourself from yourself so much that your momentum of fretting and fussing about the future is carried into the meeting so that you cannot fully concentrate. You cannot stay in the moment because you have practiced stepping *out* of the moment. Thus, your performance is diminished, you are rejected, and you move backward financially.

Then, in the same example, imagine that you are willing to ignore the meeting, you stay focused upon the present moment for three weeks, living fully, being alive, perhaps making a few plans about the meeting, then, you simply extend the habit of *being alive in the moment* and you have great vitality in the meeting. Your natural creativity pours forth and you win the meeting.

These kinds of examples you can find throughout your life, where you plan, fret, and fuss about the future, and then arrive at the future and have some difficulty engaging it when it has become the present moment. So, think long and deep about these areas.

❖

When you make an attunement to the Divine Realm, fully engaging the present moment becomes extremely important. For, as you sit trying to feel the love of the souls, or the majesty of God, and you notice that you are *not* having that experience, you can begin to think about how to make some adjustments so that in a *future* moment you can have a deeper attunement. Over time, this creates a habit of *squeezing* the present moment, and when you arrive at the future moment in which you planned to make a deeper attunement, you are in the habit of squeezing rather than *opening*. Thus, the future moment of attunement is also flat. And the future moment after that, and after that. You extend the habit of losing the present moment and you take that habit into the future by repetition.

If, in each present moment, you embrace that moment, you open your heart, you live that moment fully, then, in the next moment you will do the same, and the next, and the next. You develop the beneficial habit of opening rather than squeezing.

❖

When you think deeply, you can understand that *there is no future moment.* There is only the continuum of successive *present moments* that you arrive at one after another, at least in the human experience within time.

If you could understand that there is only *an eternal moment* that "expands" in all "directions," then you would know that *this* moment that you are living now *is* the eternal moment, and, it is the most precious moment in your life. If you cannot feel that and appreciate it now, then the next moment will not seem precious enough, and the next, and the next. This is a very important key to fully living human life, to investing yourself in life, and to the awakening of your full capacity to feel significance, purpose, and meaning in the present moment, which then opens the way to feeling greater joy.

❖

Another important aspect of creating joy in your life is the management of your criticisms of others. There needs to be a certain understanding in any moment of the eternal now that the way that you designate "enemies"—threats to your experience of life from other persons—will be an important factor in the presence or lack of joy.

You will not physically line up enemies and kill them, but, you "kill" yourself in a way when you look at another and say, "This is a *bad* person." Through that, you make a choice not to have a warm regard for that person because you see that person as a threat.

By condemning that person, you are killing a spark of joy in you that could be kept alive simply by saying, "I do not like the *behavior* of this person, but I recognize that there is the magnificence of God Itself within this person that I can value and love, even from a distance."

By lining up enemies, whether it is persons, or events, or places, or situations, and criticizing and condemning them, you cut off important aspects of your inner experience and thereby establish patterns that gradually squeeze the joy out of your life. The more that you criticize, find fault, and condemn, the more you squeeze the joy.

Conversely, the more that you are willing to remember that the negative expressions of others are temporary confusions, and the magnificence of God lives within their being, then the more you open up an avenue of greater joy. You then see all about you, not threatening enemies, but *humans similar to you in their striving to bring goodness into their lives.*

So, this is another factor to monitor in your awakening to more joy.

❖

The final focal point for this moment is to suggest that you find a way in each day to establish *a light in the darkness.* Most of you have done this instinctively, or intuitively, but occasionally you forget how to do it. So, this is a reminder.

Light in the darkness means that you have a belief in something that you *never* condemn, criticize, demean, and pull down. It could be a belief in a certain person, a certain truth, a certain impression of God or the souls. This belief gives you a focus for your *idealism*.

For many, it is difficult to use a living person as this light, for most presently living persons do not *constantly* manifest perfection. Thus, sooner or later they will disappoint you, and you will tend to lose your light, or your idealism, or your sense of *perfection* that has been represented by the person.

From this, you can see the great benefit of the human conception of *God*. Since God is invisible to you, then God can never disappoint you by obnoxious behaviors. So, if it pleases you, and if you are not adverse to the human *religious* conceptions of God, then you might say, "God will be my light. No matter what happens, God will always be perfect, and I can trust that. I can believe in that. I can cling to that in times of darkness and despair."

Or, your light might be as simple as a belief in *truth*. So, you might say, "If there can be truth, then there will always be perfection. Even when humans do not manifest truths, I can believe in truth as a perfect entity, or a perfect reality. And, I will always return to it. It will be my light in the darkness."

For some of you, already, your light has become *love*. This is a bit delicate to speak about, but, if you understand that love is *more* than a human *emotion*, then you can say, "Love is my light. Today I may not *feel* love, but love is *more* than a feeling. It is a force.

It is an energy. It is an eternal reality, and I believe in it, and I always shall. It shall always be my perfection, my light. No matter what happens in my life, no matter how negative and dark it might be at times, I commit to the belief in love as my light in the darkness."

Establishing an *ideal* as your light in the darkness is a powerful way to have joy, even when there is pain, and suffering, and fear, and sadness, and despair. During such challenges, you can return to your belief in your ideal, you can hold it as holy, and wonderful, and pure, and perfect. When there is darkness, you can return to your light to feel the upliftment, the comfort, the stability, the joy that comes from realigning with your highest ideal.

❖

Now, some of you have had difficulty idealizing anything. You have found nothing that seems pure enough and perfect enough for you to idealize.

If that is your path, then most likely you are healing patterns from your past lifetimes—patterns of doubt, skepticism, condemnation, criticism, and, most likely, strong criticism of yourself. So, you would need to say, "It is not that there is no light in life, that there is no pure, perfect aspect of life that I can worship and idealize. It is that I have temporarily lost my capacity to *see* those areas, and to *believe* in them."

In such a situation, you might need some assistance from others. When you see others who have strong faith and believe in an ideal, in something pure and wonderful, befriend those persons. Draw them out. Ask them to speak to you about what they see, what they believe, what they feel. It is not that you would force yourself to walk their path, but you might learn some of the ways to be flexible within yourself so that your idealism, and honoring, and idolizing, and worshiping can become part of your life.

Many ones can do this with *nature*, for usually, unless there is some disturbance such as a storm or earth quaking, nature is quite friendly, and it does not insult you. It does not criticize you, or condemn you. And, there is a certain purity in the natural world, particularly in the domesticated animals that can be loved, even if other humans are turning against you. That is why many of you find your light in the love of domesticated animals. You love their purity and that gives you a thing to believe in when all else crumbles about you.

❖

It should be clear to you that if you do not build a belief in a "light" focus—an area that you idealize and worship—*before* challenge falls upon you, then, most likely, you will not be able to do it while you are overwhelmed by despair or turmoil. So, you need to *plan ahead.*

Let us say that you are taking a long journey through the desert. If you do not plan ahead and take some water, when you are in the midst of the desert, you will die of thirst. Before you journey into difficult negative experiences, you need to be building an idealistic vision, a focal point for your highest idealism. At times, this requires *imagination*, not *logic*.

Let us say that you decide to believe in *God* as your focus of idealism. Yet, you have no evidence that God actually exists, and, at heart, you believe that there is no God. You need to say, "I know that it benefits me to have a focal point of idealism. It brings me joy and comfort, and light in the darkness. So, I will *pretend* that I believe that there is a God."

As you try to pretend that there is a God, you will be inclined to try to imagine the *nature* of God, the *form*, the *structure*. If you become involved in this kind of mental activity and you do not create a *feeling* of holiness and veneration about God, then, when you have a great challenge, you will not be able to feel the comfort of your perfect ideal. If you are in great despair and you try to turn toward the light of God, all that you will have are your imaginings of a *form*, the intellectual ruminations upon the nature of God that you were focused upon. There would be no feeling of love, light, inspiration. So, it is not so important to *believe* intellectually. It is important to *feel*.

If you would say, "I love apples," and you create a powerful *feeling* about apples where you would say, "Apples are divine, apples are eternal, apples love me," and you strengthen that feeling by a day-to-day *worship* of apples, then, when you fall into despair, even though an apple is a small reality, you have built such a strong *feeling* of holiness and eternalness about apples that the feeling can help you bring light into the darkness.

You could, perhaps, do this with a beloved person if you are flexible and do not become disappointed with some of the person's frailties. You might say, "I believe in the holiness of the love of my mother as my light." Then, even if she makes death, you can still idealize and worship the purity that you feel in her.

❖

This area of creating joy by idealizing, worshiping, does not depend upon *facts*, or your perception of what you might call "reality." It depends primarily upon *feelings*.

You may have noticed that there are some human *leaders* in earth of whom, objectively, ones would say, "They are not truthful. They are not sincere. They are not kind. In fact, they use their followers quite dishonestly." Yet, you can see some of their followers who see in such leaders, a holiness, a purity, a perfection. Those followers have such strong *feelings* of goodness about their leader that they are benefited.

From the objective point of view, you might say, "The *facts* are that this leader is dishonest, and the followers of this one are being deceived." In this case, the followers of this one are not focused on facts.

They are focused on *feelings*. From their point of view, they have a focus of worship and idealism that expands their hearts. It helps them bring joy and light into the darkness.

❖

If you have no focus of idealism, then, for your greater joy, you *need* one. And, *you* must decide what that focus will be. You could worship a brass monkey, and, as long as it helps your heart to open, and it represents a purity that you can *feel*, and that you believe is never diminished by any human challenge, then, you would have great benefit.

The wisest focus for your idealism is a purity that *you partake of.* Imagine that you call your focus of idealism, "the Forces of Life." Then, if you imagine that *existing within you*, not separate from you, not distant from you, then, in times of darkness, you can make a deep feeling of honoring, worshiping, celebrating that light *within you.* You can *feel* the wonderful joy and the inspiration of it.

Most humans will tend to shift their idealistic focal point somewhat as they mature through the years. The key is simply to *have* a focal point of idealization and worship, no matter what it is. If you choose a one that seems *true* to you, then it is more effective in bringing light into the darkness. If you can find nothing that seems true, you will simply need to choose *something* so that you have the experience of idealizing, worshiping. That is a very large key to joy in your life, particularly when you are sad or challenged, or in the midst of turmoil in your personal life or in the world. You will always have that focal point to return to, to draw the love from, and to give the love back to.

So, each day, ask yourself, "What is my focus of light? What do I worship and honor?" And, if it is not present *in the moment*, then you need to continue to work diligently until you can bring it into the moment. It is not enough to think about it in the past, or anticipate it in the future. You need it in the present moment, in the eternal moment.

This is the great mystery that human ones have explored through the ancient periods in which you were trained to bring forth the entire focus of your attention upon the holiness of the One God. In this lifetime, you need to say, "What then is my idealistic focus? What is holy, and how will I *feel* it, and rejoice in it in this lifetime?"

❖

Questions and Answers

NOTE: The following question was asked by a woman who needed clarity about different emotional patterns related to the death of her young child. The Guides' answer shows how negative emotional patterns can block the experience of joy, and how the healing of those patterns opens the way to joy. Their answer also reveals some unique ways in which souls interact with living people to help them. The specific details given about one of this woman's past lifetimes illustrate how challenging patterns from past lifetimes are worked out in the present.

QUESTION ONE: My only child died of cancer when he was five years old. In the weeks and days before he died, he seemed to assume an amazing state of calmness, acceptance, and wisdom that was an inspiration to me. I felt in a sense that he provided me with the strength and guidance to get through the process of his death. Occasionally, when I am sad, or frightened, or lonesome, I sort of call on him and feel his presence in a loving and reassuring way. Also, I have had some dreams about him over the years. Some dreams are sort of reunion dreams in which we are together briefly, and the feeling of love is incredibly overwhelming and blissful. I also have a recurring dream, which is almost a nightmare, in which I am living my life and I remember after several months that I have a child whom I've left somewhere and forgotten about. I have these incredible feelings of horror, and shame, and guilt, and the only way I get through that is to wake up. Would you tell me about the significance of these feelings and dreams about my son? Also, has my child come into human life again?

THE GUIDES: As you can sense, these are extremely important areas for you to continue to sort through in a gentle manner.

First of all, you might imagine a *god* who would see humans struggling and would briefly descend into earth to show them a new path. This is a bit symbolic, but, in certain ways, it describes the soul of your son.

His soul would not have chosen to come into human form in this lifetime had it not been for certain important areas that *you-as-a-human* were to master in this lifetime. And, the inherent tendency in the child's physical body that would bring about the early death was chosen by the soul of the child.

So, you could say, "I am so blessed that a god has descended into earth to teach me and guide me." His was a soul, you might say, that was far beyond the ordinary human manifestations, and his only purpose in this life was to touch you for a brief period of time. There was no desire on the part of his soul for the experience of life in human form for itself. You could say that here is a Christ-like being, from the human point of view, "sacrificing" for you.

That is a mostly accurate way to think about this relationship so that you can continue to celebrate and rejoice in his soul. This does make a wonderful focus for you for idealizing and worshiping in this lifetime.

Now, as you might expect, the challenging dreams and negative feelings about this area have to do with past lifetime experiences. You abandoned this child in a past lifetime in which the guilt and the shame that you experienced would torment you until your death.

You have healed most of those patterns before this lifetime. It is not now a large challenge, but, it has nagged at you. That, combined with some of your self-diminishing habits, has made it important to occasionally stir up some of the old feelings of guilt or shame so that they can be vented.

Usually, it is enough simply to sort through them in a *dreaming* experience. It is not so much that you need to consciously occupy with them in the waking

life. But, if, in the waking period, you notice some
thoughts and feelings of this kind, bring them
forward and fully experience them. Say to yourself,
"These are the final threads of these negative
patterns, so I will feel them fully, live through them,
then release them and go forward, knowing that there
is no truth in the feeling that I am failing, or that I
have not fulfilled important responsibilities."

Now, it can be of some benefit to briefly imagine
the small "emotional splinter" in your side from a past
lifetime that has festered, and that you are now
healing. Look to a lifetime in the past in the Central
Asia in which, as a female human being of privilege,
you were quite pampered and indulged by a wealthy
father and mother. In that lifetime, there would come
for you the mating by agreement made by the family,
not by you.

You were quite physically beautiful. You were
quite intelligent, radiant. You would be considered a
great "prize." But, the one chosen for you in marriage
was rather repugnant to you. The marriage was a
monetary, political arrangement.

In the first year of the marriage, there would
come the birth of a female child to you. After the
birth of the child, you were quite youthful and
reckless. You would be quite rebellious, and
mistreating of your mating one.

Eventually, you would make a romantic liaison
with a youthful male one. After a few years of that,
you would see your child as a burden, an impediment

to your own joy. And, being one of mostly selfishness and self-indulgence, you would simply abandon the child and your marriage one. You would take a portion of the family wealth and you would flee with the youthful male one.

Eventually, you would have a great sense of disappointment in your new mating one and you would abandon him. Then, you would go from one mating relationship to another.

During these periods, you would experience great emotional sadness and pain. You would begin to focus upon the loss of your child. And, after the seventeenth year of the child's life, in great turmoil and torment, you would say, "If only I could return to my child, I would find peace."

You would try to accomplish that, but, the child would reject you in hatred. From that, there would be a lifetime of feeling that you had ruined your life. You also believed that you had severely harmed your child. These emotional areas were so painful that, even until your death, they would haunt you.

In many lifetimes after that, you made certain healings, and most of these old patterns are now healed. So, in this lifetime, this is not a large challenge, but simply an area to occasionally think about.

Mostly, you need to feel blessed by the presence of the child in your life in this lifetime. You need to feel honored that a soul of this exalted nature would come forth into human form to love you and guide you. And, the love from that soul does continue to pour into you in every moment of your life.

This soul will not choose to enter human form again.

❖

NOTE: The woman who asked the following question wanted to know how to bring the joy that she experiences during meditation into her daily life. The Guides' answer focuses on ways to expand the experience of joy even when there are some negative thoughts and feelings that need attention.

QUESTION TWO: I realize that in some visceral way, not just in my head, I am owning and knowing that joy is my natural, normal state, and not these other illusions that I pretend about being overburdened, overstressed, and so forth. And this feels like a really big opening for me. I have felt the joy in the eternal realms during meditation. Would you help me anchor this solid knowing in my time and space illusion when I deal with my life challenges?

THE GUIDES: The key, of course, is the returning to the thought, the feeling, and the belief in *the true goodness and joy*, in spite of any evidence to the contrary. But, you have learned enough to know that if you do that without giving enough attention to your negative feelings of burden, pressure, sadness, pain, and suffering, then the focus upon the truth simply becomes a denial of the challenge of the present moment.

So, you will need to continue to wallow in the feelings of sadness and pain when you have them.

Then, after you have released the negative feelings, and you wish to transcend them, you can call upon the inner patterns that you have diligently created through the years in attunements. Those patterns bring you a releasing, a freeing from the negativity so that, emotionally, you can begin to feel the perfection of God, and the joy of that.

This is accomplished by a slight "inner movement" that shifts you away from the darkness toward the light. These are the areas that we have previously spoken of as *an idealistic focus*, a central focus of *worship*, that you use to bring light into the darkness. Emotionally and intuitively you have, through the years, built a rather strong sense of this focus.

This releasing of negativity and the shifting to the idealistic focus is the ultimate key to joy. It is the key to returning your conscious awareness to Divine Perfection. And, it is done by desire, intention, will, which you have practiced in many ways. So, you might say that the key to "anchoring" this experience is to continue the kinds of adjustments that you have been making for a long period.

Those adjustments, essentially, revolve about honesty with the negative feelings of burden, then the willingness to live through them, if possible share them, then the releasing of them with the knowledge that they have not diminished or damaged your being.

At times, negative feelings can stress and strain the physical body if they are not lived through and released. They can frighten you personally. But, they cannot diminish or damage your *being*.

Most of the time, you know that, and you feel it. At times, you can doubt it. But, always, through your diligence, you return to that central focus of love, idealism, purity, perfection, and, to the best of your ability, you try to align your thoughts and feelings with that. So, you might say that already you are anchoring the joy in your human *self*. It is only necessary to continue the focal points, and the ways that you are living.

The feeling of being burdened is also related to a lack of receiving from others. Imagine that you are climbing a mountain. You are climbing with partners. But, you are very prideful, and you believe that the only true mastery of a mountain is gained by climbing without assistance from anyone. You come to a very difficult passage on the mountain. Even though there are partners beside you who could help make that passage less difficult, you insist upon doing it yourself. And, you do. But, at some cost to you. You are drained. You are temporarily exhausted because you stubbornly mastered alone.

That pattern is beneficial in certain ways. But, if you wished more joy, you would have asked for assistance. There is joy in doing it alone, and you can rejoice in that. There would be *more* joy in doing it with assistance from others.

So, you might say that one aspect of anchoring the joy that you experience in attunements, beyond the many ways that you usually work with yourself, is to let others help you more in daily life. This is an area that you are familiar with, and you have made some inroads. But, the joy would be greatly expanded if you would give a bit more attention here.

❖

The Guides' Closing Teaching

If you ones could see your own patterns, you would either rejoice, or recoil in horror. For, you would say, "At times, I am a royal person who has come into the streets and is wallowing in the mud. I have forgotten my nobility. I treat myself as though I am dirt in the street."

If you saw yourself doing that, you would be so startled. But, when you do that inside your human *self* through self-diminishment, you believe that you have valid reasons to condemn yourself. You believe that you have valid reasons to criticize yourself as a failure, or as inadequate.

Each day, it would serve you well to say to yourself:

> "Let me step back from my usual patterns, in the name of more joy, and make certain that I am not drawing myself into the mud of self-diminishment by condemning and criticizing myself. For, I *am* of nobility. I am in the lineage of God Itself. I am a child of God, and I need to honor and cherish my present human *self* as a most precious being."

Now, of course, this does not mean that you pretend to be perfectly satisfied with all of your thoughts, feelings, choices, behaviors. You will see areas that do not please you. So, you can say to yourself, "Here, in these areas that I find to be negative, I am a noble one, acting *without* nobility. Let me change this area. But, it does not make me less noble, less of a child of God, because I have temporarily created some negativity."

Each day, come toward yourself with a conviction that *you are a most wonderful being*. When you see yourself doing less than wonderful, you can feel sad about that, or disappointed, or even angry with yourself. But, do not condemn yourself as an inadequate or unworthy person. Simply say, "I am not making the choices that reflect my true nobility, and I wish to make some changes. I will make those changes with love and respect for this wonderful being that I am."

If you come to visit a queen on her throne, and she has her dress crooked and wrinkled, you do not say, "You are an ugly hag. You must straighten your dress." If you do speak of the wrinkled dress, you speak with respect, respecting her nobility.

In the same way, when you speak to yourself about errors, or areas that you wish to correct or change, do it with respect, with kindness toward yourself. For example, you might kindly say to yourself, "I notice that I have cursed my friend in anger. That is not such a noble way to communicate.

In the future, I will think more clearly before I speak to my friend."

When you take this kind and respectful approach toward yourself, there then comes a feeling inside you that would say, "My thoughts and feelings may not always be perfect, but I am so committed to my noble station as a child of God that I will constantly and patiently make adjustments in love, in kindness." This alone will increase your joy in life many-fold. So, it is very wise to take this attitude.

❖

In this moment, imagine that you are standing in front of yourself, and yourself sits on a throne, and is noble and wonderful. You see some wrinkled clothing on you, and you feel that this is certainly not noble. But, you know that yourself is not the clothing. *You are the wonderful being within the clothing.*

In this moment, as we embrace you, as we love you, know that you are not the clothing of temporary thoughts, and feelings, and behaviors that you have accumulated in this lifetime. You are the noble being within that clothing. If that clothing does not please you, then you can change it. But, no clothing will change *you*. No temporary negativity will diminish your being. Your being is magnificent. Your being is wonderful. And, the more you *feel* that, and *live* it, the more joy you will have, day by day, throughout this lifetime.

And, for this time in earth, the speaking is ended.

❖ ❖ ❖

CHAPTER 6

The Sixth Reading

The Guides' Opening Teaching

Within the present moment, there is a certain *pricelessness*. As the present moment passes, the opportunity to receive the priceless treasure of this moment shifts to the next moment.

There are Divine Forces that are *always* perfect, that can be received by you ones in *any* moment. But, in the future moment, *you* will be different in your human patterns. Thus, you might say that *the present moment* is the last moment for you to experience the Divine in this particular form, or shape, for, in the next moments, you will have "aged" slightly. You will have made certain different experiences that you did not previously have.

You can see that you are "expanding" moment by moment, day by day, through the years. Even though you can feel, within you, "I am always *me*," in certain ways, in terms of your personal experience, you are not the same "me" from moment to moment.

For example, you cannot directly experience your present life from the point of view that you had when you were twelve years old, for that perspective has passed. Soon, more years will pass and you will have the "old" you receding into the distance of the "past." These areas are *the multiple interplay of the illusionary nature of subjective experience within time.* And, all of it is the "game" that you ones are playing at the present moment on earth.

If you do not train yourself to savor each stage of the game, there will be a certain sense of *lack* in the future. After your death, the perfect vision of *you-as-a-soul* will take note of a kind of "insufficient experiencing" that you created by not fully engaging the moment in your human life.

This would be as though you are sent to a university by your father to learn the Astronomy, and you sleep through half of the classes. When you are tested, it is clear that you did not learn fully. Thus, you are sent back to school.

It is not so much that you ones are sent into earth to *learn.* You are actually sent to *rejoice,* to experience Divine Joy while alive in human form. But, since you ones have not fully awakened to the true majesty of human life on earth, you are still "learning." You are learning to awaken. So, until you awaken, you could say that you are in *school.* When you do awaken, you will realize that you are in *play.*

It is very difficult for most human ones to understand that *the only reason for coming into human life on earth is to experience joy*. At times, joy is so far from your experience that it seems that the purpose of life is to struggle.

Believing that the purpose of life on earth is to learn is a certain kind of *distortion*. For, the original intention of the souls was not for humans to learn. In the first stages of human life on earth, humans were consciously aware of their Divine nature, and they experienced the full and complete joy that is the purpose of human life. Thus, they did not need to learn.

Then, as the downturn of human societies was initiated by human selfishness, humans forgot the true purpose of life on earth. So, in very complex ways, through the ages of time, you ones have been re-engaging the study of "being human," lifetime after lifetime. And, still, you have not *fully* learned, so your lives are a chore at times. Life seems to be *lessons*. When you fully learn, life will not be lessons. It will be *play*, and *celebration*, and *pure joy*.

❖

When you ones have long periods of moments strung together in which you feel inadequate, unworthy, unfulfilled, lonely, frustrated, frightened, angry, then you create the belief that you have new "lessons" to learn. As you *define* those lesson, then you must learn them. But, in learning those lessons, you create new ones. Then, you believe that you must learn those. On and on it goes, becoming human burdens through many lifetimes.

All of this could be stopped in an instant *by grasping the eternal perfection of you in this moment*. If you do not grasp it in this moment as the present *self* of you at this stage, then that particular moment of opportunity is gone. However, in the next moment, you have a new opportunity, being one moment older, and slightly different. A year later, you have a new opportunity, and you are a year older, and you are *more* different in your human habits.

In this manner, your human life gradually leaks away. Most of the present moments slip past without you seizing upon the true majesty of yourself, and the true magnificence of life in earth. And, gradually, there is built, once more, just as you ones have built in many lifetimes in the past, the belief that life on earth is difficult, challenging, frightening. It is not that you *always* feel that, but, that is a very strong pattern that each of you has created in the past and you are trying to heal it in the present.

❖

The key to healing is always *the present moment*. No matter what you are doing in any moment, there is always the possibility in that moment of awakening to the *truth*. And, the truth is: *There is only goodness in all realms of existence*. If you ones perceive a *badness*, that is your creation in alignment with other humans who are confused.

Day after day, the creation of *joy* is not simply to make you feel better about life and to eliminate experiences that do not please you. But, you might say that, *seizing upon joy is the key to awakening to eternal truth.* The same could be said for seizing upon *love*, seizing upon experiences of *perfection*.

So, in the simplest way of looking, you could say that joy, love, perfection—all of the experiences that you would call *positive*—are perceptions of *the truth that there is goodness in all of life*. All experiences that you would call *negative* are perceptions of *human distortion*.

What this means is that, the more that you capture joy, as with love and perfection and the other areas, the more that you are moving toward truth. So, it is not simply a self-indulgent desire to have more pleasant experiences that launches you ones in a search for love, harmony, perfection, and joy. It is your innate impulse to grasp the underlying goodness of life, to become aware of it in the human moment in which you are living, and thereby transform your personal human experience. As you do that, you begin to add to the transformation of the human distortion that has made human life on earth *seem* difficult, frightening, or painful.

So, you are playing a part in a very large drama, and you are sharing the drama with every living human. But, as you can observe, many living humans play a rather negative part in the drama at times. They bring forth resentment, anger, blaming, condemning—many negative areas—and they propagate that for long periods. That continues the illusion that there is *badness* in the human world.

Others constantly strive for the love, kindness, compassion, goodness. That stimulates a movement of human energies toward truth.

Once you realize that the pursuit of joy, of goodness, is not simply a selfish pathway that makes you feel better, but is a contribution to the transformation of distorted human creations in the physical world, then you can understand that joy has a very large purpose in human life. It is a very "high calling," so to speak. And, it is very beneficial for you, and for humanity as a whole.

These areas are difficult to see when you ones feel that you are simply one small individual amongst so many, that your life has so little impact because there are so many other human lives. That is a temporary distortion in your perception because you do not perceive the way that you touch into, and feed, every living human. You cannot perceive the hidden connections that join you to every soul. You do not see that an extraordinary cosmic drama is playing out within you, and around you. Mostly, you see your own "smaller" life, and often do not see your connection to the larger reality.

❖

You might say that the pursuit of joy is a "holy crusade." It is a primary purpose of human life on earth. It is a pathway that not only can enliven you, making your existence on this earth more fulfilling, but, it is a contribution to the awakening in human life of an awareness of Divine Perfection. So, it is certainly a noble cause, and one that extends far beyond what you often perceive as your small individual world. And, it is a cause that, if you take it as a goal in your life, along with a passion for truth and a desire for love, can accelerate what you accomplish in this lifetime—magnifying it, extending it, radiating it out far beyond your subjective experience.

These are very important layers of truth, and these suggestions can point you in a beneficial direction. Then, it is up to you to extend your thoughts and feelings along these lines until you learn to perceive these deeper truths for yourself.

❖

Questions and Answers

NOTE: An important aspect of creating joy in life is creating experiences of love. In the following question, a man in the Retreat group asks about a challenge he has in feeling the love of the Guides, and he also asks about feelings for a woman he knows. The Guides' answer reveals the importance of opening emotionally to both joy and love. The answer also touches on perceiving spiritual guides.

QUESTION ONE: The general theme to my question is "opening up." I do feel the need to monitor how much I share with others. I can accept your teachings about opening to love on an intellectual level, but I have not allowed the love to truly penetrate my heart. For example, I have a new woman friend and I feel an emotional blockage with this lady. And, I cannot feel the love that your Readings say my spiritual guides are giving me.

Would you please give me some information regarding this issue, and your teachings about opening to love?

THE GUIDES: When you adopt a certain *focus* in life, which becomes either a philosophy, or belief, or a feeling that it is *good* to live in a certain way, then there is great benefit to you. And, if that focal point has wisdom in it, it can serve you for an entire lifetime. However, if that focus is "thin," if, as a belief or a philosophy, it is filled with some human confusions, it will usually wear out rather rapidly and you will find that it does not sustain you for long. Then, you will simply put it aside and seek another focal point.

When you are in the midst of a transformation, as you are—and remember that you are transforming only *your personality patterns*, not your *being*, for your being does not need transformation—then it is wise to benefit from beneficial beliefs that help you in the transformation. If we would say, "All male ones are quite crude and insignificant, and there is no hope for them," that would not be a wise belief for you to adopt during your transformation period. For, you need to feel how wonderful you are in order to continue with the important adjustments that you have been making.

Now, if we would say that you are wonderful as a human *self*, that is not simply a teaching. That is a *truth* about the goodness of your being.

You need to continue to sort through what you take in as teachings from ourselves, or from any source, and decide for yourself what is truth. It is often difficult to know what is truth. But, when you continue to examine, and question, what you take in, you become wiser, and more quickly can you look at your thoughts, feelings, beliefs, teachings, philosophies, and more accurately *feel* the truth of them, or, the lack of truth. This is the *process* that you are now involved in.

Work with the words spoken by ourselves, and, if you feel truth in them, then continue to follow our suggestions and that becomes your present philosophy. But, it should be clear to you that this is not the philosophy of a large numbers of humans at the present time, in terms of these particular speakings that we do.

In relation to your new female friend, you could say that this is similar to loving the alligators. Imagine that you are extremely fond of them. You would not expect many others to share your interest in alligators. If you take one of your pet alligators and you rush toward your new friend saying, "Love my pet," you could expect her to run away.

The key in communicating your philosophy to others is *sensitivity to the other person*. No matter how passionate you are about the alligators, you must observe that the friend that you rush toward is frightened of alligators. So, your next step is to determine how frightened she is.

In this case, as we look at the patterns of this particular female one—and remember that the alligator symbolizes your beliefs about spiritual guides, about which there is not widespread public agreement in your society—we would say that her fears are moderate. So, if there is ongoing communication and interaction between you ones, and you share your spiritual beliefs, and ideas, and philosophies in a patient way that is sensitive to her moods and responses, then it does appear that, in time, there could be satisfying interactions and sharing of interests. This *potential* lies in the future, so you need not fret about it for the moment.

Now, to speak about your awareness of our love. Let us say that there is smoke in your room. And, although that smoke has no *hard* form, you can see it because it is white against the transparent air.

Then, imagine that you have some *transparent* smoke—which is a gas without odor. You cannot see the gas. If you would say, "There is no gas in this room," and you go to sleep, you will eventually die. The gas will kill you. Whether you *believed* in the gas or not, you are dead.

You could say, "Intellectually, I believe in a force of love pouring into me from my spiritual guides, but I cannot feel the love." But, whether you believe in that love or not, you *are* loved. The love is a *reality*, but, it is "invisible," just as the invisible gas.

If you would say, "It would please me so much to feel this love from my spiritual guides," you can begin by acknowledging that the love is "transparent." Thus, you will need to give it some "color." If you have a gas and you give it a color, then you will be aware of when there is gas. If you are willing to believe that the love of ourselves constantly pours into you, but it is transparent and you wish to give it some color—something *tangible* by which to recognize it— you could add some color by practicing *creating the emotion of love with other humans.* This experience makes love tangible because you clearly feel it— perceive it—inside of you.

If you did not directly *feel* that love inside you, then you would not know that there is such a thing as love. Love would remain transparent. But, when you love a human, even though love is transparent, you now feel it and thus you can perceive its reality. It now has a "color"—a tangible reality—subjectively to you. So, you can confidently say, "There *is* a reality of love, for I have felt it."

Had you *not* felt love at all, you could argue for the remainder of this lifetime, saying, "There is no such thing as love. I see no love, I feel no love, therefore, there *is* no love." So, the experience of loving other humans makes you familiar with the *reality* of love.

But, the truth is that *the human emotion of love* is a "small" reality. It is a tangible human experience that "represents"—and you ones have no other words here to use but the word, "energy"—it represents the *energies* of love that are Divine. Those Divine Love Energies are eternal, while the human *emotion* of love is temporary, for emotions constantly change.

You can say that these Divine energies of love pour into you from ourselves. They pour into you from the source that you would speak of as *God*. By practicing perceiving the *human love*, which is an *emotion*, you sensitize yourself to the *Divine Love*, which is an *eternal energy*. Then, at certain times, when you are very still, and quiet, and receptive, you can sit in a silence and the "transparent" energies of Divine Love that we constantly pour into you can be sensed by you as a kind of "inner movement."

At first, this might be experienced as a feeling of *calm*, or *peace*, or a feeling of *emotional warmth*. Eventually, you can have a feeling of being *nurtured*. Then, in time, you can have a strong feeling of being *profoundly loved*.

But, if you have not practiced receiving love from other humans, even though you are willing to give that love out to others, it can very difficult to align with these transparent energies of Divine Love. That lack of *receiving* human love would be the nature of your present blockage.

Now, if you look about in your world, you will see that most humans have the same blockage, some to a lesser degree than others. And, even those who are extremely loving and sensitive, even those who are willing to receive love from other humans, can often go for long periods of time without actually feeling the love of the souls coming into them. So, this is not only your blockage. It is the blockage of most present humans.

The key to becoming aware of Divine Love is always to begin with the *human* love. It involves working with your various patterns that, in the past, tended to block the human love.

We would say that you are doing quite well in this area. And, more and more, when you make the silent attunement, and you can be receptive and passive, you should begin to feel the first inklings of the transparent love that is pouring into you from ourselves.

❖

NOTE: One of the most difficult obstacles to joy for many people is a sense of unworthiness that they create about themselves. In the following question, a man who was dealing with difficult challenges in his life asked how to deal with his self-criticism. The Guides' answer can be helpful for everyone working with feelings of unworthiness.

QUESTION TWO: In my journey toward joy and fulfillment in my life, I seem to be experiencing a blockage involving a lot of self-criticism and self-doubt in this present period. Would you give me some specific ways in which I can overcome this blockage?

THE GUIDES: First of all, you must allow for the difficult circumstances and experiences in the outer world that you are now passing through. Even to those of great confidence, these would cause some self-doubt.

Next, try to distinguish between your *inner habits* of self-doubt, which you will need to continue to work with patiently, to bring forward, live through, share, and release, and, the feelings of self-doubt that are related to the present disappointments in your daily life in the outer world—feelings that will simply pass as the disappointments pass, as you adjust to the loss, or the challenge in various situations. At the moment, you are particularly vulnerable to the *habits* of self-doubt because they are being exaggerated by your negative feelings about loss and challenge in the outer world. So, it means that you need more than the usual tenderness and gentleness toward yourself during this period.

When you notice that you are having the doubts of your worthiness, take a few moments alone to severely condemn yourself. Imagine that you are the worst male one on this earth and everyone dislikes you. No one will hire you for employ. No one will wish to be a mating one or a friend to you. You will have a miserable life; you will make a miserable death. Whenever your feelings of unworthiness arise, do this with those feelings for five or ten moments. Wallow in the exaggeration of these negative thoughts and feelings.

Then, say to yourself, "This temporarily has *vented* some of my habits of self-diminishment, for I can do no worse than this in condemning myself, in using my imagination to imagine the worst. And, I have just lived through the worst negative thoughts and feelings about myself, and, *I am undiminished and undamaged in my being.* I now *release* all negative feelings."

Then, it is time to build the *truth* in your thoughts and feelings. You may need to write this out and read it to yourself when you cannot feel it. This is as though you are giving a sermon at the pulpit but you have lost your belief in God. That does not matter. Your job is to inspire others, no matter what you personally think or feel. So, in this segment of the inner process, you are the pastor to yourself. It does not matter if you believe that you are inadequate, you *must* give an inspirational sermon. It is your duty to your flock—yourself.

So, you write out the "sermon" to yourself. It must begin with this: "I am a magnificent male human being walking on this earth." You always begin in that way, for *that is always the truth*, whether you can feel it or not. You write this out.

Then, in those moments after the venting and releasing of your negative feelings, you read this statement to yourself in all seriousness, pretending that you believe in it. You give your best sermon.

You can extend beyond that initial statement and you can add many other truths about yourself, such as, "I am extremely intelligent. I am extremely idealistic and sensitive. I care deeply about life and all humans. I am extremely loving and nurturing. I have such a great capacity for bringing goodness into this earth by my own choices, my own actions."

Add to that list and write a full sermon. Then, in your moments of self-diminishment, first, live through the negative feelings about yourself, vent them, and release them. Then, give your sermon of truth to yourself. This is a process that you can commit to, no matter how you are feeling about yourself, and it will bring you great benefit.

Now, since you have had consistently had difficulty in *receiving* from others in this lifetime, you lack the accumulated upliftment that you would have gotten through the years had you allowed others to more fully celebrate you. Non-consciously, at times, you deflected others' love, their approval, their appreciation. Either you were too busy doing and giving, or, you were too busy thinking instead of feeling.

You are now making adjustments in these areas. They are much looser than in the past. It is as though you have put a great wall about your house to keep out robbers. Then, you discover that it keeps out friends. So, you begin to make some openings in the walls and the friends begin to come.

Continue in this area. Have the courage to seek out those who are sensitive, who are kind, who enjoy giving, who enjoy appreciating others. Show them that you *need* to receive, you *need* to be appreciated. Always do this gradually. You need not rush, nor shock your personality by trying to move ahead too swiftly.

Of course, being accepted professionally and otherwise has a great impact upon your feelings about yourself. And, at this moment, you might say that you are not being accepted enough. So, whenever you feel that you can manage it, in terms of time and energy, find those sensitive professional ones that you can go to with whom you can share your wonderful gifts, and, particularly, to receive their appreciation.

If you would say, "I will start a foundation that requires millions of dollars and years of time, and it will be wonderful serving others, then, I will feel appreciated," that might not be so wise because so much complexity in the physical world would need to be overcome before the project would be completed and you would begin to feel appreciated. But, if you would say, "Here is a grouping of children who need sensitive, kind adults to volunteer to help them for brief periods each week," and you go and you lift them up, and you see their smiling faces, then you will immediately know that you are appreciated.

If you do a task for a friend, or if you give to individuals in different ways, while you are paying attention to those persons, you can also invite them to appreciate you. This can be done in very small steps. The key, of course, is the willingness to *ask*, which has been difficult for you in the past.

Like many humans who love others deeply, you are more than willing to *do for them*, but less than willing to ask them to *do for you*. Always, this will be an important core of these complexities about self-diminishment and the awakening to your true magnificence. Since the "stakes are high" now, in terms of the challenging situations that you are presently grappling with in your life, you are now willing to do whatever is necessary to lift yourself, to see your magnificence. So, now is the time, as you can see, to take a stand and open this area.

❖

The Guides' Closing Teaching

Let us look now at a certain "pragmatic" view of life that is quite popular for many humans at this point in time. This view would say, in effect, "If I can *see* it, then *it exists*. If I *cannot* see it, then *it does not exist*." There are many ramifications of this viewpoint which, essentially, would say that only that which is *perceptible* to the physical senses is real. If this view is followed to the extreme, then "invisible" realities, such as *love*, do not exist, for you cannot perceive them with your five senses—sight, sound, taste, touch, and smell.

Most of you understand that you must go beyond this limited view of life in order to experience the full joy in your life. So, at times, to expand your viewpoint, you might say, "If I can *feel* it, then it exists. If I cannot feel it, perhaps it does not exist." However, this view also has some limits. If you feel *love*, then you can believe that love exists. If you do *not* feel God, then you might believe that God does not exist.

In addressing the reality of God, you must take your view of life even further. You can say, "In the past, since I could not *feel* God, then I believed that God is not real. But, if I can *imagine* God in an intelligent way, then I can eventually *feel* the presence of God, which I believed did not exist." So, *feeling can be extended by imagination.*

Next, you can say to yourself, "If I can bring forth my innate *intuitive-sensing-ability* that is not short-circuited by my intellect, and not overwhelmed by my smaller feelings, and I align that with feelings of *idealism*, then I can begin to *sense* what I cannot *see*, and what I cannot *feel*. I can go beyond the limits of human perception and emotion. In doing that, I will begin *to extend my perception of reality.* And, eventually, as I experience the fullness of *all* life, I become as a god in earth."

This *extension of perception* is difficult for most humans to understand and to achieve. To move toward this, you would need to say to yourself:

> **"I am learning to extend my perception *beyond* my five physical senses, and beyond my thoughts and feelings. I am learning to *intuit*, to sense in ways that transcend my limited human perceptions, thoughts, and emotions."**

This difficult area for humans to achieve is a most *personal* area. Each individual must discover in their own way how to use their power of intuition. We can only point to this area and describe it for you in human words. The actual experiencing of it depends upon the choices made by each individual in the way that they live their daily life, and in the time they spend in attunement to the Divine. But, the continued opening of the heart, and the stirring of greater joy and love, will help anyone who wishes to pursue the opening of their inner capacity to intuitively sense the spiritual realities of life.

Each day, you ones ordinarily focus upon your physical perceptions, and your thoughts and feelings about your life in the physical world. If you are willing to take even a small period of time each day in which you focus upon opening your *intuitive-sensing-ability*, then you can extend and expand your world in a way that will bring you joy and fulfillment for the remainder of this lifetime.

❖

Imagine that you are doing that in this moment. You are ignoring your ordinary thoughts and feelings. As you do that, you can experience a kind of inner expanding and an extension of your inner sensing in a way that goes beyond your thoughts and feelings.

Give yourself to that growing inner sensing in this moment. And, as you do that, we say to you: *The extraordinarily loving forces of God Itself are penetrating you now.*

Allow yourself to extend your inner sensing beyond your thoughts and feelings and you will begin to know how deeply loved you are. You will know that the Divine Love of God Itself sustains you now, and forever.

And, for this time in earth, the speaking is ended.

❖ ❖ ❖

CHAPTER 7

The Seventh Reading

The Guides' Opening Teaching

We would now direct your attention to the experience of your human *self* within the physical world, and suggest that this be seen for a moment as a small flea upon a dog. As that flea, you would look about and you would say, "I have a land of hair that is mine. I inhabit this land." For the remainder of your flea life, until your death, you believe that you live in a land of hair. You see only the hairs. You do not see the dog.

One of the mysteries of human life that can be exciting to solve in your own way is to wonder within yourself, "What are the hairs that I perceive in my world, and what are they upon?"

When you ones look at the physical world, particularly if you have an understanding of scientific information, you could say, "I live in a vast, infinite universe of physical objects." If you would imagine that universe as *one* hair, you could begin to realize what you actually live within. The immenseness of the physical universe can often startle you ones, but, if you would understand that universe as only one hair upon a "Divine Dog," then you would have an overwhelming sense of the smallness of the physical universe in relation to the infinity of the Divine Realm.

Now, imagine that you as a flea climb to the top of the one hair and you look about. In other words, you gain full knowledge about the physical universe, believing that with such knowledge you will solve the mystery of life. However, when you climb to the top of the one hair, you see more hairs. When you sense beyond the physical universe to the vastness of the Divine Realm, you awaken to the vastness of life—you see a vast field of many hairs. But, still, you have not seen the dog.

The challenge, of course, is that *you-as-a-soul* have chosen to create a temporary experience for your human *self* in which your human *self* will not see the dog. As you live this lifetime, your human *self* will be a flea. However, the real mystery is that—and there are no adequate words for this reality so we will continue to use this image—even though your temporary human *self* can only perceive the hairs, *you are actually the dog*. All of the hairs are small parts of your larger being as an eternal soul.

❖

Now, if you would imagine that your present physical universe is one hair upon the Divine Dog, then the challenge for your understanding is that *the rest of the hairs are not physical universes.* They are eternal realms of an extremely different nature from what you are accustomed to perceiving in the physical universe. And, among those different realities, the physical universe is quite "small."

The challenge here extends to your *imagination.* You ones can imagine billions upon billions of *years* in which there has been a certain unfoldment of the physical universe. Yet, regardless of your ideas and theories about these billions of years, the mystery here is—just as you are simultaneously the flea and you are the Divine Dog—*within your experience of time* in the physical universe, simultaneously, *you are experiencing that there is no time in the Divine Realm* that "contains" the physical universe.

You can see what a confusing situation you find yourself in as a human *self.* It is a situation in which it appears so obvious that billions of years of *time* have passed in which the physical universe has formed. This, within time, has led to the present moment in which you exist as your human *self* within your physical body. Yet, the *truth* is that all of the billions of years of time have passed in a Divine Reality in which there is no time.

Your personal experience within time needs to be respected and lived out fully. If you are a flea, then you must respect your forest of hairs and not try to abandon the forest. Yet, you might say in your human *self,* "It would be quite joyful and wonderful to truly understand the mystery of my existence in this physical universe." But, if you approach that only as an understanding of the *physical* world—understanding the origin of early matter, understanding the origin of hard bodies in space, understanding the origin of cellular life—that can be quite amusing and fascinating, but, it is the study of the hairs, not the dog.

❖

In order to break out of the limitations that are "automatically" imposed upon you ones by your physical body—your physical perceptions and your human study of the physical universe through those perceptions, linked with an ever-evolving human intellect—you need a different perspective.

Now, if this new perspective can be achieved, not only will it bring you closer to the true mystery of your existence and your life on earth, but, while you are the flea, it will bring you great joy. If you discover that you are not lost in a forest of hairs, but you are actually living upon a beautiful dog, it will make a profound difference in how you feel about yourself and your existence as a being.

The challenge for you ones is that you cannot escape the forest of hairs consistently enough to build a repertoire of experiences that grow strong enough to match your powerful convictions about the physical world that have been formed inside your body. Yet, there is a mystical path that has been taught since the beginning of human existence on this earth in which the human consciousness is "elevated" into an experience of the Divine Realm.

❖

In the teachings of the mystical pathway, you first come to know the human *self* that you are. Then, you learn the origin of the *life* that inhabits your human *self*. Then, you discover what occurs to the human *self* when that "life force" leaves the body at physical death. This becomes a foundation for your consciousness to occasionally "spring free" from the limitations of human perception framed within a physical body.

At the present time, the actual process of attaining this expanded, or "transcendental" perspective is quite varied amongst humans. It is often dictated by past beliefs, and traditions, and trainings that have been handed down through the human generations.

This is similar to preparing to go to a very important ball. Imagine that you have been invited to a ball in which the President of the United States will appear, and, he will be there to honor *you*. If you respect the President, then you could imagine no more important public occasion.

You wish to dress very well for this occasion, so you go to your wardrobe and your mother would say, "Here is a costume handed down from your grandparents. They thought it was quite beautiful so it is suitable for this occasion." You are horrified because the costume is out of style, and it is too small for you.

Many of the traditional human teachings about the mysteries of life that served earlier generations are too "small" for presently living humans. The human intellect has grown much "larger" than it was when those early humans fashioned their teachings. Those teachings are now out of fashion because they do not take into consideration the extraordinary *complexity* of your present human world, a complexity that did not exist in earlier times.

When those traditions were initially created, human life on earth was extremely simple. Thus, ancient teachings may not fully prepare you ones, within your present complex society, for gaining the transcendental perspective.

However, at the present time, most of you ones have "memories" *beneath your conscious awareness*, of transcendental experiences that you have had in quite a few past lifetimes on earth. You now have, hidden within you, the experience of the extraordinary bliss that you had when you became consciously aware of the Divine Forces of Life beyond time and space. So, in a sense, you can now become your own teacher by discovering deep truths that are hidden within your present *self*.

We are not saying that you must avoid the ideas of other persons, or their writings, or teachings, or traditions, that inspire you. But, rarely, will those lead you to a *consistent* direct experience of the Divine. So, you might say, "Here is the old costume that has been handed down. It is too small and out of date, but, I can tailor it." You can adjust the older teachings to fit your present needs. But, at some point, you might realize that they do not take you far enough. They leave you longing for a greater direct experience of the Divine.

When that occurs, those who lack confidence in their own inner wisdom and true magnificence will feel, "Then, I am lost. These truths that I have searched out do not bring me an experience of the Divine. Therefore, there is no way that I can achieve that experience." Yet, for such ones, the truth is: *The way lives within themselves.*

❖

Each of you has non-conscious memories of certain inner adjustments that you made in past lifetimes of earth that can spring free your conscious awareness from human limitations. By drawing upon that inner wisdom, and by making certain adjustments, you can untie the "knot" of human consciousness and free *your perceiving point* from the physical brain. Your human *self* consciousness can spring free from its encasement in the physical body.

When you accomplished this in past lifetimes, it brought you the Divine bliss, the extraordinary joy and love that is always your experience as an eternal soul. With patience and persistence in attunements, you can bring forward your intuitive-sensing-capacity to move toward such experiences of the Divine in this lifetime.

So, in your present life, you might wish to *trust*

that you already have the knowledge within you that is needed to spring free your perceptive viewpoint, to untie the knot of consciousness, and to experience the perfection of the Divine, as least as far as that can be done while you are still alive in a physical body. It is a matter of trusting your own sense of how to adjust your thoughts and emotions, trusting your own wise impulses, in terms of how to release restrictive inner patterns, and how to open yourself and give yourself to the Divine.

This is not an area that can be taught in words. We can only bring forth words to encourage you to experiment with ways to draw forth your intuitive wisdom that lives deep within you.

The simplest procedure is to dedicate brief periods of silence each day to an attunement in which you practice using your *intuitive-sensing-ability* that is usually obscured by the great volume of thoughts and feelings about your life in the physical world. Those thoughts and feelings usually fill your conscious awareness moment by moment, and that is what makes it difficult for you to feel that you have this intuitive-sensing-ability.

If you make this attunement each day, patiently, learning to ignore your normal thoughts and feelings about your life in the physical world, then, even if you do not immediately have a profound experience of the Divine, you will have a steady inflowing of peace, and calm, and joy to nurture you throughout your life. And, if you continue to open emotionally, and apply yourself lovingly to your daily attunement, there can occasionally be the bringing forth of your intuitive-sensing-ability in a way that will lead to an extraordinary experience of the Divine that can inspire you for the remainder of this lifetime.

The key here is to trust that the wisdom that you need to draw upon lives *within you*. It does not live in a teacher. It does not live in a religion, a tradition, another person. Your profound wisdom lives within you, within the depths of *your human self energies*.

Again, we are not discouraging you from aligning with teachings, persons, writings, religions, traditions that inspire you. If you need those areas, then take them up and they can be beneficial. If you wish to climb a mountain, but you are too weak, and you are not trained well enough, then you can climb with an expert who puts a rope upon you and pulls you up to the top.

After you have reached the summit with that assistance, there is a certain meaningful achievement that serves you. But, you have not *mastered* the mountain through your own choices and actions.

In certain lifetimes, you ones have been lifted spiritually by a teacher, a master, who helped you experience the Divine. Then, when the master would make death, you could no longer achieve the summit.

In this lifetime, after many lifetimes of essentially being "students," you ones are now becoming a teacher to yourself—if you wish to be. If you desire, you are now able to say to yourself:

"I am prepared to have the joy of Divine Bliss in my life. I am willing to commit to daily attunements in which I will trust the inner wisdom of myself, aligned with the wisdom of my soul and other souls. I am prepared to move forward with sincerity in these attunements every day. That, combined with honor, honesty, and love in my daily life, will eventually lead me to a direct glimpse of God, and a direct experience of the Divine Realm."

This can be a wonderful joy to bring into your human life.

❖

Questions and Answers

NOTE: For some people, the joy that they have in doing their favorite activities in daily life can be diminished when they start to believe that their life after death will not give them the chance to continue to explore those activities. This was the case for the mature man who asked the following question. The Guides' answer paints a fascinating picture of the way that joy is expanded after death.

QUESTION ONE: As I progress to the later stages of my life, I wonder more and more about the experience of *dying*, and going into a different consciousness and a different realm of existence. I have a concern that the creative endeavors that give me joy in this life, such as the perception of beauty, the creation of beauty, and the revealing of beauty through music and painting, will not exist in my experience after death. I enjoy the process of learning about the endless complexity of artistic expression, and the peeling off of the layers of the onion of learning, getting closer and closer to a perfect expression. I worry that any existence that I'm going to have after death cannot, according to the teachings that I come into contact with, have anything equivalent to this because the realm is one of perfection, and of all knowledge and bliss, which is wonderful, but that doesn't seem to include the ability to penetrate mysteries and complexity, to solve problems, to create beauty that wasn't there before. Would you tell me, is it boring on the "other side," or, are there things in the spiritual existence that are equivalent to the things I just described?

THE GUIDES: There are many layers to this "onion" of life. You can begin with the *outer* layer, which you might imagine as *the unmanifested forces of God Itself.*

Imagine *the most wonderful experience* that you have ever had. Then, imagine it *infinitely expanded and multiplied in **goodness.*** This would be a crude way of imagining the unmanifested Forces Of Life.

You need not probe too deeply here with your intellect, for it becomes confusing. But, you could say that, just as you desire this deep satisfaction of exploring the beauty of music and artistic expression in this lifetime, the Unmanifested God Force would desire a "hobby," crudely speaking. That hobby would involve *the creation of souls.*

Then, you could say that the *souls* would desire a hobby. Their hobby would involve *the creation of the physical universe and human life on earth.*

Then, humans would desire a hobby. Their hobby would be *creativity,* which involves the creation of music, art, literature—all of the artistic areas that humans have created.

The challenge to your intellectual understanding here is that, from your human point of view, all of these "hobby levels" of reality—from the Unmanifested God Force, through the eternal souls, and to humans—appear to be *separate* from one another. That is the illusion that humans must learn to see through in order to perceive the truth.

Imagine that you go to the marketplace, and a naïve person who knows nothing about marketplaces sees you buy a bread and some milk that you put into a basket with many other foods that you have purchased. The naïve person would say, "This person has a bread and some milk." They cannot understand that you have *groceries*. The bread and milk are part of your groceries.

Human ones cannot understand that the joy that you ones find in your specific hobbies, or your expressions artistically—the bread and milk—are part of *your vast soul experiences*—the groceries.

It is very important to your soul that your soul infuses a passion for creative expression into your human *self*. Therefore, certainly, you would not expect that important focal area of creative expression to vanish when you put aside your physical body.

In relation to creative expression, what *will* vanish is a certain human sense of *limitation*, which you ones equate to *discovery*. But, *true* discovery is not *overcoming limits*. It is *expanding potential*.

For example, in the early, "pure" periods of the

human habitation of earth, there was an impulse to create what you now understand as *music*. During that period, music did not exist as physical sound created by humans. So, humans began to create music through "song" from human voices.

Later, in one of those early periods, you personally, as a one in a small grouping who would be a portion of the "temple singers" in a land that has now slipped into the sea, would experience extraordinary joy in the human song made with the voice. Then, yourself and a small grouping, began to wonder if there could be joy in other kinds of sounds.

You ones, mostly inspired by your souls—for in those early periods the *human choice* was not a predominant factor, so you ones mostly responded to inspiration from your souls—there was the early invention of the first stringed musical instrument. And, you had a passion for playing that instrument.

After your death from that lifetime, you would go forth and *you-as-a-soul* would see the great joy that your human *self* had created in playing that instrument. Even though the musical instrument did not *physically* exist beyond the physical world, *the passionate joy* in your human *self* from playing that instrument *was taken into your soul*, and, it was *extended in extraordinary ways that multiplied your human joy in music.*

Then, there came a certain *mystery*, for, not even your soul, nor God Itself, knew exactly what your human *self* would do in the next human lifetime with your passion for music.

In this lifetime, that passion has been brought forward in your present human *self*. And, through your human choices, instead of *playing* music as you did many times in earlier periods, you have become passionate about the *recording* of music electronically and mechanically.

When you make your death from this lifetime, again, the creative passion for music and artistic creation will go forward. And, even your soul does not know what your human *self* will choose to do next if you return to earth in the future when there are even more extraordinary musical opportunities available to you. Upon your return, you may decide to invent musical instruments that have never before existed.

As long as you can understand that there is no *separation* between the realms of life, then you can understand that human life does not separate you from the Divine Realm. And, the joy that you have in the human realm cannot be lost in the Divine Realm. Simply because the instruments in the soul realm are not made of *physical matter*, that does not mean that there is a vacuum, or a void, or a lack of the same kind of experiences and patterns that so fascinate you with present music and instruments.

We cannot find adequate words to portray the magnificent nature of the Divine Realm. We can simply assure you that it is not empty. It is not simply a *static* perfect feeling. It has to do with *unfolding experiences*. It has to do with certain types of "experiential movement." And, in a sense, it has to do with certain types of *objects*. The fact that those objects are not made of physical matter does not make them boring, or uninteresting, or less mysterious.

This can be a troubling area for you to think about. So, simply say to yourself, "At the present time, my imagination is limited by my human perceptions. But, I am an extremely creative person. And, if I apply as much creative passion to imagining what will occur after death—particularly in terms of creative passions—then I can come somewhat close to imagining the truth about life after physical death."

If you take the same passion that you now put into music and painting, and occasionally put that into a creative imagining about your experience after death concerning these creative focal points, then you should come fairly close to a kind of envisioning, at least a feeling, or a sensing, of the true reality of all of this.

❖

NOTE: The man who asked the following question wanted information about musical abilities he had in past lifetimes. For most people, a joyful life involves integrating artistic expression into daily life. The Guides' answer gives fascinating information about this man's past lives, and his present artistic abilities, showing how past lifetimes and present choices determine how much joy will be experienced in the present.

QUESTION TWO: You told me in a personal Reading

that in past human lifetimes on earth I have been a musician, and that I could have more joy in this lifetime by mastering and playing a musical instrument. Please discuss some past lives that I have had as a musician, and please give me some advice and guidance on what musical instruments I could master now with ease and proficiency that would provide me with the most joy in this lifetime?

THE GUIDES: In looking at the patterns of the past lifetimes, the most joy that you experienced in the past was with the playing of the *organ*. However, you must recognize that this may not bring you the most joy in the present.

The playing of the lute was also quite satisfying for you in the past, as was the piano, as well as an earlier musical instrument of Greece that no longer exists. In the present, it is not so much of importance the particular instrument that you choose, but the *feeling* that you take to the playing of an instrument. But, generally, you might be better served with instruments that are played by the hands and not by the mouth. We are not saying that you should avoid the wind instruments if you become interested in them, but, more likely, you will be attracted to those instruments that are played by the hands.

Now, in looking at the past lifetimes in which you expressed through the music, it is wise for you to assume that since you have a fondness for success and mastery in this lifetime, then that has been important to you in the past. That "ambition" has helped you become adept in many human expressions. So, you can assume, quite accurately, that when you gave yourself to music, you became very successful in the writing of it, the playing of it, the touching of other humans through the music. You might say that this is a chapter written in your book of the past.

In this lifetime, it may not be your primary purpose to touch others through the public performance of music as you did in the past. It may simply be an important addition to your present life choices, if it pleases you to add the music.

Now, looking backward in time, in a portion of the Austria in the past, we see a predisposition to the music that was very strong in you at an early age. Without much encouragement or prodding, you would be drawn to the piano and the violin. And, there would come a passion that would endure throughout that lifetime. You would be recognized early for your genius, and there would come great favor and joy in many ways as you would be respected and even idolized in certain areas.

This does not mean that those two particular instruments would immediately fascinate you in this lifetime. But, if you found enough interest to approach one of them, and you assumed that you have a certain innate mastery already achieved in the past, and you felt no ambition or no need to be *perfect*, or to *prove yourself*, then it would be similar to returning to an old friend with whom have had many joyful experiences. You do not see the friend often, but occasionally you return to renew the joy.

When you look at the musical area now, your

present perception is, of course, clouded by the complexity of your present life. In earlier periods of time, there was less distraction in the human world. Choices were much simpler. There was even a sense of a great *divinity* about music, a sense of spiritual awe. Often, the music was related to a profound love of God in you.

In the present, you can perceive that, for your society, music is mostly *entertainment*. It is not that this is wrong, but, it is a bit more superficial. It is related to *human emotion*, rather than to a celebration of the Divine. So, since your passion now is mostly a celebration of the Divine, it will be difficult to link music with that in any *public* context.

However, you can link music with the Divine in a *private* context by stirring up sensings and feelings from earlier lifetimes in which you were transported to the Divine Realm through music. You would not expect to attain that profound depth of spiritual experience in this lifetime, but, any instrument that draws you, that you wish to experiment with, that you indulge a bit in and learn to play, might inspire yourself, through the beauty of the music, and would echo many areas of completion and mastery from the past, and, perhaps, occasionally lift you to a sense of the Divine.

But, in this lifetime, the stronger sense of the Divine for you will come through human love, not so much through the music. So, you might say that you will put this impulse toward music "in your back pocket," so to speak. In your front pocket will be many other important areas that you are pursuing in this lifetime. If you wish to add the music, then there will be benefit. If you choose *not* to add the music, there will be no diminishment of your pathway.

If you *do* add the music, then *you* must decide what draws you, in terms of the kind of music, and the particular musical instruments that you would focus upon.

❖

NOTE: The following question, about how and why a soul chooses a particular birth family for the individual, is a question that many people have. In response to that question, as asked by a man in the Retreat group, the Guides help clarify the importance of the birth family, and they give a broader understanding of how family affects the person's overall experience of joy.

QUESTION THREE: Both of my parents are still alive. They are 75 years old and have been married for 55 years to each other. I have a sister who is older, and a brother who is younger than me. We are all very different. My sister carries around a lot of anger and unfinished business. My brother is an introvert who just kind of doesn't deal with much of anything. And, I have a pretty good relationship with my parents. My question is, why did I choose this particular family this time around? What was I sent here to learn?

THE GUIDES: The birth family context for you in this lifetime is secondary to the mating area, and the more *chosen* family experience with others. This is not to say that the birth family is unimportant.

The sense of distance, or lack of importance that you might feel at times about the birth family is not so much ignorance on your part, or a failure to have an open heart, but simply a kind of "artifact" of the choices made by your soul before this lifetime. This is a very complex area, and difficult to put into words, so we will use an image for you.

Imagine that you go forth into a field and you are attacked by a bull. You are seriously wounded by its horns. Years later, you completely forget the attack, but, each time that you go into a field, you are very frightened. Then, you avoid fields.

You have had some very dramatic emotional pain and suffering in the birth family area in a few past lifetimes that are fairly close to the present lifetime, in terms of time—you were gored by the "bull" of family challenge that severely wounded you. The strongest pain in the birth family area had to do with violence and atrocity committed upon your family during a time of war that caused you unbearable emotional pain related to family experience. You cannot consciously remember that "attack," but, the tendency to avoid the "field," the family area, has been brought forward to heal in this lifetime.

Since there were important purposes that your soul wished your present *self* to accomplish *outside* of the birth family relationships in this lifetime, you might say that your soul did not chose a birth family in which you would have an overwhelming sense of connectedness, and be so deeply tied to them emotionally that each time that they were wounded you would feel severely wounded.

It is not that there is a lack of love for the family here, for there have been some very strong love experiences with them in other past lifetimes. But, *you-as-a-soul* understood quite clearly that there would be certain dynamics within this family that would most likely unfold in this lifetime as patterns that do not invite a great depth of feeling of family love. So, your soul took this as an advantage that would leave you free for more independence to find deeper love on your own, to go forth with a sense of self-determination, and, even, at times, a sense of detachment from the birth family.

Now, a small thread of that sense of distance from the family, of course, would be your old patterns of protecting against emotional pain in general, and over-emphasizing your masculine qualities of strength, forcefulness, determination, and so forth. Had your soul chosen a different family for different purposes rooted in *very deep* family love, then, even your present tendency to master life with masculine abilities of intellect, courage, strength, and determination would not have diminished an extraordinarily strong emotional attachment to family, even to the point of, in your earlier years, being so "homesick" when you left the family that you would feel compelled to return. Those would have been the "alternative" patterns that your soul could have chosen for you had there not been important reasons for having the birth family that you have in this lifetime.

So, you might say, "If I manage to stimulate love in a deeper way in *this* family, then I have made a large accomplishment." And, in many ways you are teaching your own family, to the extent that you are willing to learn about each one of them and love them. Yet, they each have their important purposes for being in this family, and, you have yours.

In your earlier years, those different purposes of the family ones coincided somewhat. But, even as a child, you sensed that you would move in a different direction. At times, you would even have the feeling, "I do not truly belong here."

This feeling has to do with many complex patterns, but, mostly, it is due to the kind of non-conscious "aversion to family" that we have described that is related to the terrible emotional pain in the family area in certain past lifetimes. This is also related to the choice of your soul not to force you to face that aversion "head on" in this lifetime by causing you to be overly-attached to family.

Instead, your soul chose to let family be a sort of "peripheral" area while you focus on areas that your soul considers more important, such as, discovering how to love a female one, discovering how to stand by in intimate relationships in loyalty instead of fleeing in fear of suffocation, discovering many areas that would not have been appropriate to work with in what you would call your "family of origin" in this lifetime.

So, consider any improvement that you make in the family relationship area to be an extra, a "bonus." It is an addition to more important aspects of your life that you are exploring and mastering apart from family of origin.

❖

The Guides' Closing Teaching

In this moment, consider that there are many different "movements" within the present patterns of the personal *self* of each of you. This would be similar to coming to a grand ball and watching the dancers. You would notice that some dance passionately and eagerly. Others would stand in the corner not dancing at all. Nevertheless, *they all hear the music.*

At this point in time, you could say, "I have my own unique path in life. And, I have my own unique responses to these particular teachings that I have been receiving in this grouping. If I notice that any of the teachings do not touch me, then I will put them aside for a while. With those teachings that *do* touch me, I will expand upon them."

Each individual, in their own way, will decide what the important inner movements are that are occurring in their thoughts and emotions at this time. You will each decide what to do about those inner patterns. Those are the unique choices that you ones make about how to dance at the ball. And, you make *different* choices at different times, according to what you believe is best.

Then, no matter how you address all of that, we can say to you ones, if *greater joy* is what you desire in your life, if you truly desire to wield the healing power of joy, then the direction of change needs to be toward *loosening and expanding emotionally*, not tightening and protecting.

The emotional loosening applies to all ones, no matter what different individual choices they might be making. No matter how they choose to dance at the ball, the music that they all hear is the pattern of expanding emotionally, which applies to all of them equally.

There is nothing wrong with tightening and protecting emotionally. It simply is not that joyful.

❖

For this moment, imagine that everything that would trouble you, frighten you, burden you, has suddenly been taken away. Imagine that a beloved father has smoothed all of your challenges, has healed all of your pain and suffering. So, in this moment, you are entirely *safe, free,* and *loved.*

In this moment, there is nothing to protect against. There is no threat, no danger, no badness. There is only the beloved eternal souls rejoicing in you. And, as you stand within that love, you realize that, "It is time to open my heart and allow this Divine Love to pour into me."

For this moment, imagine *perfection* all about you, *goodness, beauty, harmony,* and, Divine loved ones who are rejoicing in you without cease.

As you learn to feel this more and more, it will become a pathway of great joy for you throughout this lifetime.

And, for this time in earth, the speaking is ended.

❖ ❖ ❖

CHAPTER 8

The Eighth Reading

The Guides' Opening Teaching

To continue on toward a deeper understanding of the healing power of joy, it is now necessary to look more closely at the area of *Divine Joy*. This is an area that is so difficult for the human mind to grasp.

This is as though you have come to the land of China and it is very difficult to understand the ones who live there because there is a different language spoken. As we speak about Divine Joy, in your human *self*, the words are registered by your brain and assimilated into the conscious knowledge that you have accumulated from your childhood to the present. And, in the country of you ones, that knowledge is "encased," or conceptualized, in the English language.

All of that makes a kind of "mask," or a shield, or a screen, around your inner experience because it is so important to you ones to think and communicate in the English language. That takes precedence over other sensations, and other sensings of *other realities*, particularly the reality of Divine Joy that could possibly be *intuitively* perceived by you, but cannot be accurately *thought* about in words and language.

What this means, then, is that, if you have a strong desire, in a sense, to perceive the "language" of your soul—not only the way that your soul would, what you call, "communicate," but also how your soul experiences itself *within Divine Joy*—then it is necessary to put aside your screen, which is your *language*, which lives in your *thoughts*. For, when you contemplate the life of your soul, your soul's existence, your soul's language, and you begin to have *thoughts* about all of that, you have the screen.

No *thought* will ever bring you ones an *experience* of your soul. No thought will ever reveal to you the true nature of your soul, and its existence, and its language. Yet, if you have no thoughts at all about this, then, usually, you will feel lost at sea, for you are used to stabilizing yourself and defining yourself through your thoughts.

❖

It is quite uncomfortable for most human ones to give up thought. You ones have a stubborn insistence upon letting the mind dominate you throughout your day, and even during your periods of attunement. There is a certain kind of fear to put aside the thinking that has stabilized you for all these years. But, if you choose to make gentle attunements each day to practice *ignoring* your thoughts for a period of time, then, even if you do not entirely eliminate the screen of thinking, you can make cracks in it so that you can peer through to the other side of life, to the reality of your soul participating in Divine Joy.

So, when you are pondering your soul and you wish to awaken more to an awareness of your soul, it can help quite a bit to consider that your normal thoughts, which ordinarily serve you quite well, are a screen that needs to be parted, not eliminated. You might find it impossible during attunements to entirely *eliminate* thinking. But, you can begin to find cracks in the thoughts by learning to *ignore* your thinking.

Then, you can establish a sense that *you are not your thoughts.* You need not be dominated by thinking. You can turn your *attention* away from your thoughts, peering through the thoughts, or seeing beyond them.

Now, when you do this, essentially, you are shifting your inner perceptions to more of what you might call "feelings." This is not so much what you know as ordinary *emotion.* It is an *intuitive feeling-sensing.* You do have an *intuitive-sensing-ability* within you, but, most of you are so unused to drawing forth this ability that, at first, you do not even know that it is there.

Imagine that you are very poor, but, you have been given a large plot of land. You have the land, but, you still feel very poor. If you knew that there were great amounts of gold beneath your land, then you would be quite different in your attitude toward the land. You would know that you are wealthy in *potential*.

As you think about your inner intuitive-sensing-ability, there needs to be a certain *feeling* that you have a great potential within you, beneath your conscious awareness. You need to grow an expectation that you can actually begin to become aware of that powerful inner ability that is an extraordinary intuitive-sensing-ability. Then, in your attunements, when you learn to, in a sense, peer through whatever thoughts you are having, there will be the discovery of the golden treasure of that intuitive-sensing-ability that lies hidden beneath the surface of your ordinary awareness.

You may not immediately notice your intuitive-sensing-ability, but, at least, you can now know that it is there. Earlier, with a lack of knowledge, you may have told yourself in your thoughts that you do not have this powerful intuitive-sensing-ability. Now, even if you simply think about having such an ability, your thoughts will be telling you that this golden treasure does lie beneath your "land" of conscious awareness.

❖

Imagine that you come to a fair to have great joy, but you believe that you have no money for the exciting rides. You can have a bit of joy by simply being at the fair. But, if you had money for the rides, you would have more joy.

Then, imagine that you remember that you have a great deal of money in your pocket. Now, even though you have not taken the money out of your pocket, you know it is there and you have a strong joyful feeling.

When you make an attunement and you peer through your thoughts, or float above them, and you simply *know* that you have a deep intuitive-sensing-ability within you, then, even if you do not bring it forth from the "pocket" of your non-conscious awareness, you can still feel quite joyful.

If you stand at the fair, knowing that you have money in your pocket, but you do not take it out to go on the rides, the joy remains, but it is small. If you spend the money and have the rides, the joy is large.

If you go beyond simply *knowing* that you have an intuitive-sensing-ability, to actually *using* that ability, then the joy becomes much larger in your life and in your attunement experience.

Most ones are still a bit confused about this area, for you have not yet had enough direct experience of your intuitive-sensing-ability. So, we will show you a simple method that you ones can use to draw this treasure forth into your experience in an attunement period.

In this method, you will need to use your thoughts somewhat. But, the thoughts will not be focused upon your ordinary human experience in the physical world. Instead, they will be focused upon the use of your intuitive-sensing-ability to begin to awaken to Divine Joy. Then, in time, using that ability, you will bring forth the occasional experience of the life of your soul, the language of your soul, the existence of your soul.

❖

As you begin to use this attunement method, consider that you will need to "prime the pump." In other words, you will say, "I now am ready, in my gentle attunement moment, to use my intuitive-sensing-ability." Since you do not know *how* to use that ability, you might believe that you must sit in silence waiting for it to spring up on its own. That might occur, but, it may take a long period of training. If you prime the pump, then it can occur more quickly without so many years of training.

The way that you prime the pump is to begin to think about your soul in a certain way that is not too far from the *reality* of your soul. That is how you begin the method of stimulating your intuitive-sensing-ability to eventually sense your soul in its ongoing experience of Divine Joy.

Now, the *words* that you will use in thinking about your soul are, of course, distant from the actual *reality* of your soul. But, there are certain powerful words that you can think that are close enough to that reality that they can prime the pump for your intuitive-sensing of your soul. The first words to use would be these:

> **"My soul has a *Divine Majesty* that can fill me with a feeling of *perfection* and *Divine Joy*."**

Using these words in your thoughts at the beginning of your attunement will echo the actual experience that your soul is having at all times. The words are not the *experience*, but, at least, they point your awareness in the right direction.

In this part of the attunement, you would say these words in your mind, calmly, gently, knowing that you are inviting your intuitive-sensing-ability to begin to move toward the actual experience that your soul is having in that moment of time. In reality, *you* are your soul having the experience of Divine Joy "outside" of the "smaller" experience that your human *self* is having in that attunement moment, but your human *self* is blocked from a conscious awareness of the experience that your soul is having.

Using these words will initiate a certain kind of "reverberation of energies." As you sit within your small human experience, beginning to open your intuitive-sensing-ability, you can understand and feel that, in that moment, your intuitive-sensing-ability is the *link* between *you-as-a-human* who is having an attunement experience, and *you-as-a-soul* who is having a majestic experience of Divine Joy, an experience that your human *self* is not consciously aware of. It is your intuitive-sensing-ability that can eventually bring that soul experience to your conscious awareness.

By virtue of willfully choosing to use your freedom to create such word-thoughts, you begin to stimulate your hidden intuitive-sensing-ability that you rarely notice. It is as though you are taming a large tortoise, and the tortoise assumes that you are dangerous, so it keeps its head in the shell. You hold out some food, and gradually the head comes out of the shell.

In the same way, gradually—and this would take a period of time—by seeding the attunement moment with these particular words that we have suggested, your intuitive-sensing-ability comes out of its "hiding place" beneath your conscious awareness. You then can begin to use that ability to actually *feel* some of the magnificence of your soul experience of Divine Joy that you have stated in those words.

As you practice this consistently in your daily attunements, you can refine the process by formulating words of your own that you sense are true about your soul. Those new words can also point your intuitive-sensing-ability more strongly toward the soul experience of Divine Joy.

❖

In *thinking* about your soul outside of your attunement period, you ones can unintentionally create many obstacles, for the human mind is quite stubborn, and it will try to completely and fully explore any thoughts that you have. So, if you would think the thought, "My soul is tied with God," your mind will not leave it at that, but will try to fashion more and more thoughts about *how* your soul is tied to God. Your logical mind will rush ahead to discover *explanations* and *reasons*. Then, you will go off in the wrong direction, for the words, "My soul is tied to God," are not *truths*. They are a *concept* created by words in your mind.

Your soul is not tied to God. Yet, in a way, your soul is "linked" to God, but, in an extraordinary manner that is not accurately described by those words. And, the connection between your soul and God cannot be perceived by thinking those words. However, that connection can be perceived by your intuitive-sensing-ability when you can go beyond the words.

So, we suggest that, unless you are making an attunement, or if you simply need some inspiration during your day in which you wish to remember that you are an eternal soul, you do not need to think about your soul during your ordinary day. You need to think about being human. You need to think about mastering your human pathway. That way, you "save" your thoughts about your soul for *special* moments, making them more precious. You bring them forth only as a catalyst during your attunement period. It is as though you have a precious jewel that is so valuable and you wear it every day. Soon, it becomes ordinary, even though it is still so valuable. If you take it out on special occasions, it remains uniquely wonderful in your eyes.

Yet, outside of your attunement periods, a conscious experience of your soul can occasionally be brought to you by your soul. In such an experience, you will not usually say, "I am now feeling my soul."

But, in moments when your need is very great, you might notice an unusual peace and calm come over you. You might notice a stirring of a feeling of being loved, or a feeling of being accompanied in a comforting way by a loving presence.

So, occasionally, when there is great need in your heart, and when you are innocent, and receptive, and open, and you are not striving, or forcing, or pushing in that moment, your soul might bring forth a certain inspiring experience that you perceive through your intuitive-sensing-ability, even though you have not intended that, and you have not created it by your own will. However, such experiences are a bit rare for most ones.

Usually, in order to consciously experience the great joy of being *you-as-a-soul,* and to have deep experiences that can soften you, and inspire you, and encourage you in this lifetime, you will need to create the *receptivity* for that in periods of silent attunement. With daily attunements, you can continue to go forward in your human expression with more hope, more courage, more optimism, more idealism. More and more you will feel confident that you are not simply a small speck on the face of the earth that will be stamped out at physical death. You will begin to feel, more and more, the majesty of your soul expressing through you as a human in a physical form. And, in time, if you persist in your attunements, you can even feel the majesty of God Itself expressing through *you* in human form.

❖

This is the great fulfillment you can have through using your intuitive-sensing-ability to move toward Divine Joy. Using that ability intelligently, sensitively, during gentle periods of attunement each day, there can come the expansion of your awareness of all aspects of *you*, in the human world, and in the Divine Realm.

However, many ones can feel that they have too many obstacles in their daily life to make an attunement. They do not take the time to practice awakening their intuitive-sensing-ability. Certainly, that is not wrong. It is not bad. It is simply *small*.

Each day, you need to say to yourself, "What is important for me in this day?" If you declare that it is important to go forth in your occupation to sustain yourself financially, then rejoice in that, for that day is a very brief moment in eternity, and you need to savor it while you are living it, no matter what you are doing.

If you would say, "Today, human love is so important. I will pay attention to every human who crosses my path, and I will try to feel their magnificence, and feel the love that joins us," then do that and rejoice in that.

If you would say, "Today, it is very important to feel my soul," then establish an attunement period, enter that attunement to your soul, carry out the attunement experience to the best of your ability, knowing that your attunements will eventually awaken your intuitive-sensing-ability so that you can have a profound experience of your soul.

However, it would not serve you ones for your attunement practice to become *exceedingly* important in your life at the expense of your human path. Again and again, we remind you that you did not come into human form with the primary purpose of experiencing your soul. You came into human form to experience your human *self.* You *always* experience your soul beyond the physical reality, for you always *are* your soul. But, it is only for a brief period within time that you have the opportunity to be your present remarkable human *self.*

A human experience of your soul can be "added" to your life whenever you wish to add it. Think of that experience as a "bonus," you might say, in your human life. As long as you see it that way, then your inclinations toward the Divine will be beautifully and harmoniously merged with your many important human purposes in this lifetime. And, after your death, you will have the greatest appreciation for your human life as you lived it in this lifetime.

❖

Questions and Answers

NOTE: Many people experience great joy when they connect with the beauty of nature. The woman who asked the following question had such experiences, and she asked to Guides to explain why her experiences in nature were so impactful.

QUESTION ONE: I would like to ask for clarification with regard to the attunements that occur when I'm in nature, in a very easy and natural way. Often I'll be walking in nature in a very receptive state where my mind is quiet and peaceful, and my senses are awake, but quiet. Then my non-physical awareness spontaneously comes to the foreground. While my senses notice the beautiful colors and movements of the plants, ocean, the lake, or trees, there's a sense of wonder, and awe, and discovery, as if I'm really seeing all this for the very first time. In addition, there's a sense of the eternal and the temporal occurring in the same moment, and a very deep feeling of peace and completion. Would you please describe the process that's occurring, as much as it's possible to describe it, from the point of view of the souls, when I, or any human being attunes to the plants or the minerals in nature. What is it that we're attuning to? Are we attuning to the soul expressions that are maintaining these life forces? And, are there threads from past lives which would serve as a teaching in this area?

THE GUIDES: There are many threads here. We will focus upon a few.

The first thread is the mystery of the human *self* in relation to the soul, and how humans have made choices that limit the human *self* experience. The simplest way to grasp this is to imagine that you have been given a beautiful coat. It is perfect. But, as you look at it, you decide that it is too long, so you shorten it. Then, you decide that it needs more color. You sew on some colorful patches. Then, you decide to make other changes to the original gift. Eventually, it comes to be very ugly. Then, you would say, "Why have I been given such an ugly coat?" You have forgotten that it was beautiful when it was given to you, and that you made changes to it that made it less than beautiful.

In the very first stages of human life on earth, the gift from the souls—the human *self*—was perfect. The human experience of you ones was perfectly *good*. There was no fear, no doubt, no worry, no ugliness, no pain, no suffering, no negativity of any kind. You ones had a perfect coat as a gift from your soul.

Through the human lifetimes, you ones would declare, for example—and here we will greatly simplify this long period of time—"Having sexual intercourse with this person that I am attracted to is more important than bringing kindness and love to this person. I will use this person's body for my own pleasure."

This kind of *self-preoccupied* response would occur in many ones. Gradually, self-preoccupation would become stronger through a vast number of human generations until it became *human selfishness*.

Another example of such human choices would be one in which humans might say, "On this plot of land where I grow my food, if I share it with others, I might go hungry. Therefore, I will begin to keep everything for myself."

This was the human patching of the original gift of the beautiful coat. The patching on of selfishness, self-indulgence, self-involvement, would lead to a widespread human fear of loss, and a strong mistrust of others. Then, through many lifetimes, these negative patterns would lead to competition and war between large groupings. There would come to be hatred. There would come to be all of the various ills of the human world that you ones now must live through and master.

Even though, at the inner *core* of the *human-self-energy-structure*, there are still *perfect* soul energies being poured into you ones, what you ones have "wrapped around" the perfect core of the human *self*, in terms of your outward behaviors, has become more and more self-involved through the ages, and thus, more negative from the human point of view.

When you go into the world of *nature*, because of certain predispositions that you have brought from past lifetimes of earth that have to do with experiences of great joy in the beauty of nature, you can leave behind all of the burdens that humanity has accumulated through the ages. When you go into nature in a relaxed manner, you can almost remember, in a feeling-sensing way, the original beauty of the original coat of the perfect *self* given to humanity by the souls—the original *perfect* human experience in which there were no incrustations put onto the human *self* by human confusion, selfishness, and fear.

As you sense that perfection while you are in nature, you are actually opening your intuitive-sensing-ability and you sensing the perfection of your soul. You can feel that the perfection of the souls is ongoing, even though the perfection of the human *self* has been temporarily obscured. The original perfection of the human *self* has been temporarily interrupted by human choice. Yet, at the *core* of your human *self*, beneath your conscious awareness, the perfect energies of your soul still pour into you.

At times, as you release into the beauty of nature, you can sense that the perfection of the soul occurs *outside of time and space*, while the "imperfection" of the human *self* "coverings" occurs *within time and space*. The plants, the animals, the manifestations of the natural world, occur within time and space, and, in a certain sense, the natural world is the only clear and consistent reflection left of the perfection of the souls, for it is no longer that clear in certain human *self* expressions.

Now, we generalize greatly here, for there are many moments in the lives of you ones when you are kind to one another and love one another. Those are moments in which the perfection of the souls is present in your expressions. But, generally, you ones do not appreciate that, or, most humans do not make it a priority in their lives. So, the patched coat moves forward, receiving more patches, becoming more ugly. Again, generalizing quite a bit.

So, when you go into nature, you could say that you are perceiving the only remaining remnants of perfection within time and space—ignoring now the "pollution" of the natural world by human choice. And, given your predisposition and the spiritual training that you have had in a number of past lifetimes, there is triggered the strong intuitive-sensing-ability that you have nurtured in this lifetime. So, not only are you responding to the "artifacts" of the perfect souls within time and space, which would be nature in the physical world, but, you are beginning to sense the pure perfection of the souls outside of time and space.

This results in what you might call a "closing of the circle," or a unity, or a merging of all dichotomies and opposites. It is what you might call a *mystical* experience, in the sense that all of the human obstructions *within* time and space are penetrated, and the true perfection *outside* of time and space is experienced by you as you stand in nature inside of time and space.

This is a general kind of vision that you can then apply to many different aspects of your life, whether it is your own inner experience, your relationships, your teaching, your philosophy, your spiritual beliefs. Often, you can simplify the complexity of human life by saying, "I look at the world, and I look at myself, and I can see that which is less than perfect. I can see the encrustations that we as humans have placed upon the experience of life on earth, blockages that obscure the Divine Perfection. I can see what we have done within time and space to make the beautiful coat so ugly. Now, I must decide what I wish to do about that. Do I wish to take some of the ugly patches off of the beautiful coat?"

When you contemplate the true beauty of nature, and you release yourself into it, in that moment, you are not bringing any of the human imperfections into your experience. You are not bringing forth your worries and frettings, and, equally important, you are not bringing forth your desires, your ambitions.

No matter how wonderful and perfect your desires and ambitions might be to you, they are *human creations*. And, when you are wishing to attune to the Divine, you need to *stop creating*. You need to allow God to create for you.

By giving yourself to the beauty of nature, you are distracted from your normal concerns, even your positive ones. So, you put down the many patches that you have placed upon the perfect coat of your human *self*, and you begin to see and to experience your human *self* in its true perfect form. You also begin to sense your own soul in its true perfect form.

These are wonderful, mysterious areas of experience to play with, to encourage yourself to experiment with, without a great deal of aggressive thought, or desire to capture teachings or truths. It is an area simply to indulge in.

After a time, after you have such experiences consistently and you see the benefit that they bring to you, then, you might try to capture some of these truths in words that you can give to others to help them in their confusion, their sadness and pain. You might try to suggest to others ways that they can make similar adjustments so that they can rejoice in experiences with nature.

All of this depends upon you, and your choices. But, once you have certain experiences and you have opened a door, then you can choose to lead others to that door and see if they wish to pass through it also.

❖

NOTE: For spiritual seekers, an important aspect of living a joyful life is having a sense of being connected to God. The mature lady who asked the following question wanted clarity about some ideas about God that she had read in a book. The Guides' answer gives a way to integrate a belief in God into a productive human life.

QUESTION TWO: In a class, I am studying a very deep spiritual book. It addresses our human power bestowed on us by God. Most thoughts in the book are familiar, but some cause some hesitation, such as, "You are God and God is you." I'd like for the Guides to teach me about the concept: I am God and God is me. It seems like it could be a powerful concept if I could understand the spiritual meaning and could live accordingly. If God is me, to whom do I pray? Would you please clarify this?

THE GUIDES: If you are a nurse, and you are nursing dying persons, you must give everything that you have to save the persons. But, if you come to a party given to celebrate *you*, and you insist upon nursing your guests instead of allowing them to serve you, then you are quite confused.

You must understand that the human mind can draw forth the *concept* of "unity" between humans and God, but, *temporarily*, *within* time and space, you are a human *self*, not God *beyond* time and space. Yet, in the *eternal* sense, you are woven with the Divine Forces that you would understand as God.

For the moment, your *conscious* point of view is not focused upon your soul awareness. It is focused upon your human *self* awareness. So, you could say that *you-as-a-human-self* are not God. Yet, *you-as-an-eternal-soul* are immersed in and fully conscious of the Forces of God, so, you could say that you *are* God.

You need to say to yourself, "I must be flexible enough to see *shifting contexts*. In this lifetime, I am my present human *self*, and I am living that fully and thoroughly. And, I will usually not have a feeling that I am God."

If you encounter teachings that say that you are God, even though they are true in the *largest* sense, they are not particularly *beneficial* for you. If you come to your party and say, "I am a nurse, not the honored guest of the party," that is not beneficial. You will try to nurse the party goers instead of celebrating the party. You came into the "party" of earth life, not to try to be a perfect God, but to celebrate and rejoice in human life as a unique individual.

It is very wise, in a moment of stillness, to pray to God, for, from your human point of view, you are not God. You are not consciously standing in the Divine Realm orchestrating the universe. You are not consciously maintaining the existence of the soul energies that you project from yourself as God.

However, in the largest sense, you are part of that Divine orchestration. But, again, it would not be so beneficial to spend your time thinking about that unless you need that vision for inspiration.

The greatest human teachings are the ones *that help you fulfill your human life in the most wonderful way*. If you encounter teachings that confuse you, then you must think deeply about them, puzzle over them if you wish, but, if they do not help you gain greater clarity about life, then, put them aside and seek out new teachings.

We must remind you that teachings are never *truths*. They are *human creations*, created by human *minds*. Some of them can *reflect* the truth more clearly than others, but, they are simply *words* based upon the *experiences* of humans.

The truth comes into humans as "energies," if you will, from the Divine. Those energies are not words. They have a non-physical reality that is quite different from what humans understand. However, those energies constantly penetrate humans, and when certain humans become *consciously* aware of those Divine energies through what you would call a "spiritual experience," then the humans can report the experience in words, spoken or written, that can *reflect* the truth of the Divine. The degree of *accuracy* of that reflection depends upon the *humans*, not upon God or the souls. The infusions of the God Energies and the soul energies into humans are *always perfect*. Human "translations" of those energies, put into words and brought forth as teachings, can be close to perfection and truth, or, they can be far from the truth.

So, you can assess various teachings, not upon the basis of whether they are *truth* or not—for you can rest assured that all human teachings are "un-truth"—but, you can assess them on the basis of how well they help you live a fulfilling human life. Examine the teachings to see if they inspire you to be more *kind*, more *compassionate*, more *loving*. If teachings do that, and, if they help you feel more wonderful about yourself and other humans, then it will be beneficial to use them. If they do not do that, then you would be wise to put them aside.

❖

NOTE: The woman who asked the following question had experienced an important opening during the week of the Retreat. As she explores this with the Guides, the answer to her question clarifies how the increase in joy in life depends on the choices that people make. It is not a matter of finding a way to have the person's soul increase the amount of spiritual energy that the soul is giving the person.

QUESTION THREE: This week has been absolutely wonderful and magical for me. I feel I experienced the lightness of being, and I feel more in touch with myself. I feel as if I've given myself a much awaited gift, opened a door I've been standing in front of for a long time. At the same time, I feel on the brink of something new and wonderful and exciting. Will it keep happening? What's my part in this?

THE GUIDES: You could say that you have succeeded in peeling away some ugly patches from your coat, meaning that you have gradually clarified your thoughts and feelings so that you are bringing forth the deep sensitivity that was hidden beneath confused patterns. You might say that you are more "pure" in your experience of your human *self* as a reflection of your Divine being.

Now, this does not occur by good fortune or by accident. It comes about from *choices* that you have made. So, you can rest assured that you will continue to make similar choices in the future, and thus you can expect an ongoing deepening.

Of course, doubts and fears can return at times. And, if you have complexities in your daily life in the physical world you can feel less at ease, less trusting, less loving. But, you can pass through those experiences and return to this deeper awareness of your true magnificence as a human and as a soul. *You* have brought about the deepened experience, and you should be able to return to that more and more frequently.

It is important that you understand that you are the one who has brought about this recent experience. Since your birth, your soul, and other souls, have been pouring forth more love into you than you could possibly use in any moment. So, it is not that you have now been such a good person that you are being rewarded by the souls increasing their love. It is that you have been so intelligent, so sensitive, so sincere in your day-to-day living, always striving, to the best of your ability, to bring forth kindness, compassion, and truth, that you have opened to an awareness of the Divine Love pouring into you.

Those kinds of choices have been building in you through time, but, one change in the recent period is that you are more willing to bring forth love toward *yourself*. That accelerates the awakenings that you are now having.

You could say that, in the souls' love for you, they rejoice as though they have been singing a beautiful song to you. You have so desired to hear that song, but, you have had your fingers in your ears. You have then noticed your fingers in your ears and you have taken them out. Now, you can say, "I am so joyful. The souls are now singing to me."

You could also say, "The souls have *always* been singing to me. It is because I am so wise, and I am so wonderful, that I have discovered how to make the inner adjustments that bring their song of love more fully into my heart day after day."

Now, as you might suspect, the next task in expanding your joy is to share this love more fully with others. However, even though *you* can feel the soul love within you, you must remember that many others do not feel it. So, you cannot rush at them and say, "Here is the wonderful soul love, the love song from the souls, take it in." First, you must help them take their fingers from their ears.

This is a delicate task. It has taken you years to accomplish this. So, even though you have awakened to the love in so many ways, and you have been able to penetrate the truth in a deeper and deeper way, you can understand that you could not expect, in a single moment, to help another human do what has taken you many years. You will need to continue to bring friendship, warmth, and love to others over time.

However, now you can believe in that love as a truth more fully because you have experienced it more fully. You can "advocate" it more strongly, but always with a sensitivity to how deep in the ears does a one have their fingers. If they have them very deep, you must speak very subtly over a long period of time. If their fingers are almost out of their ears, you can speak very strongly and boldly about the truths that you are learning.

We would say that it is accurate for you to say that this experience is an important turning point for you. But, the addition of wonderful new experiences will not occur automatically in the future. Just as you have created this *present* opening, you must create those new experiences in the future. And, you must decide what you wish those experiences to be, and how you will go about infusing those awakenings into your daily life. So, the work is not done, but the ability to do it has been released more fully by you into your conscious awareness.

❖

The Guides' Closing Teaching

In this moment, once again, we suggest a certain stepping back from your human experience in which you have such strong thoughts and feelings, and we ask that you imagine that you are passing through the door of death.

As you pass through the door of death, your old thoughts and feelings are left behind. You emerge from the limitations of human perception and you begin to look about. As you do that, you see with eyes that are quite new to you.

With those new eyes, first, you see what you might call a magnificent *light*, although it is much more than that.

Then, you begin to feel a certain wonderful *love* emanating from that light.

Then, with the eyes that are quite new to you, you see wonderful *beings* of such extraordinary majesty and pure love.

You realize that all of the shadows left from the human mind are filled with light. There is no shadow. There is no darkness. There is no heaviness. There is no doubt. There is no negativity. There is the extraordinary experience of *perfect love*.

You realize that you are sharing that perfect love with extraordinary beings.

❖

Even *imagining* all of this passing through death experience opens a small crack in the wall of human limitedness to your conscious awareness. And, the more you imagine it, the more the wall will crack.

However, since you are not actually making your death, the wall will not entirely vanish. You do not wish to bring down the wall of ordinary awareness. It is the wall of a "playing field" in which you are having a wonderful time playing a game. It is not time to stop playing, so you do not wish to leave the field. But, occasionally, you glance over the wall and you can see beyond it to the great celebration of those who have finished their game.

So, in this moment of time, let yourself feel that you have made the death, you have moved beyond the wall of human perception. You are part of the great Divine celebration. You are part of the most wonderful beauty, harmony, goodness, joy, fulfillment, and love. Everything that you can imagine as *goodness*, you are filled with now.

This is your ongoing experience as a soul. Simply imagining such an experience in this moment can soften you, can help you feel that your present life is not a battle to the death. It is a joy-filled game, and it is a game that you will win.

Make a gentle, calm feeling now. Nothing needs to be feared in this moment. Nothing can diminish or damage your being.

Once you know this, then the Divine comes forth and the celebration can begin even before the physical death of your body. So, for this moment, feel the love, the goodness, the joy. Let it uplift you. Let it encourage you to go forth to allow it to remain in this life, with a growing awareness of the perfection of God Itself, as it pours into you and sustains you throughout this lifetime.

And, for this time in earth, the speaking is ended.

❖ ❖ ❖

CHAPTER 9

The Ninth Reading

The Guides' Opening Teaching

We would suggest now that your thought of the moment be this:

> "I have established a strong ability, through many lifetimes, to live on this earth in great *joy*. In this lifetime, I am learning to bring more of that ability forward in my thoughts, feelings, choices, and actions as I accomplish my important human purposes on earth."

This means that you do not need to go forth and discover *how* to create joy. You do not need to add new talents to yourself. You do not need to be a different person. You already have the ability, the inner wisdom, the inner knowing, the inner sensitivity, to live a life of great joy. It is simply a matter of drawing forth those inner abilities and using them on a day-to-day basis.

We have suggested various focal points for accomplishing that. Now, we would add another for you ones.

Imagine that you are making the fishing in a pond, and you catch a fish. You could say, "How *wonderful*. I will have a delicious meal."

If you are the same person, and it is the same fish, but now you have a different *attitude* toward life, you could say, "How *terrible*. I have murdered a fish."

When you look carefully at the moments in your life, you can more and more realize that, with a negative attitude toward life, you can see *badness* all around you. With that attitude, you can create misery and emotional pain for yourself.

Or, you could see *through* the subjective perception of badness and find a beneficial aspect of any moment, even the challenging moments. This is the power of *shifting perceptions*. The more you practice this, the more joy you can bring into your life.

❖

To illustrate the power of shifting perceptions, we would ask that you would imagine that you have a large pet elephant and you wish to take a journey with your elephant. You are free to come forth and say, "I love this elephant so much that on this journey I will carry my elephant." You would have a great challenge of an overwhelming burden.

If you would say, "I love this elephant, and, on the journey, I will ride my elephant," then you will have no burden. In fact, you will have great joy because you do not need to make the effort to walk.

When you look at the burdens of your life and

you say, "I must carry them," then, of course, you have great difficulty. If you would say, "The burdens will carry me to greater insights, to greater awakenings, to greater fulfillment, they will broaden my human experience by testing my mettle, by stimulating a vast reservoir of inner strength and courage that I might not draw upon unless stimulated by my challenges," then, you are moving toward a life of mastery.

If you have a friend who is making a painful death, and it is very sad and frightening for you to be with that friend, you are free to stay away from the friend and feel burdened by feelings of guilt. You are also free to choose to go to your friend and grapple with the difficult challenges of serving the friend. This is not pleasurable for you. You would not say, "This is joyful." But, in riding the elephant of that challenging situation, you have brought forth much more courage and strength than you would have brought forward by sitting in your room and avoiding your friend.

We are not saying that you must pretend that you like painful challenges. You do not need to say, "I am so joyful that today I will have this pain and suffering." But, after you have said, "I do not like this challenge, it is too painful and frightening," and you have lived through your negative thoughts and feelings about the challenge and released them, then you can say, "I will ride this challenge forward and it will take me into more courage, more inventiveness, more determination, more willingness to master this human world, even when it is very difficult."

At times, you ones must "pay the price" for playing the game of being human, which is that you are susceptible to some temporary suffering and pain. If you run away from the challenges of life, then you do not have the great joy of playing the game fully and deliciously. If you bring forth your inner courage and strength to grapple with the challenges and master them, then you will have the great *intensity* of human experience as you joyfully play the game.

You might occasionally long for the day when there is no challenge at all, so, you can remind yourself that such a day will come after your physical death. But, while you have the extraordinary opportunity to experience life on earth once again as a human *self*, you can keep reminding yourself of the great joy that you will have by playing the game of life to the fullest in such a masterful way.

With this powerful attitude, you can learn to approach your painful challenges more creatively, even more optimistically. Not optimistic in the sense that you always expect the challenges to have perfect outcomes that please you, particularly if they involve other persons with their negative choices. But, with an optimism in which you believe that, no matter what results you might have in grappling with your challenges, you will be *benefited* in the long run by having grappled with the challenge. You can know that you will draw forth qualities in you, particularly strength, determination, and courage, that you most likely would not have brought forward had you not been challenged.

❖

The challenges for you ones are profoundly impactful areas. They are the areas that can make your life miserable. They are the areas that can blot out the joy, that can cause you to feel, at times, that there is no goodness in life, that there is only the sadness, the pain, the loneliness, the discouragement that you can feel when you are painfully challenged. So, to *fully* draw upon the healing power of joy, it is not enough to learn how to be joyful and confident, to love yourself, to love others. When you feel overwhelmed by painful challenge, it is necessary to work in the ways that we have shown you in order to have the fullness of joy.

If you would say, "I do not choose to retreat from the difficulties of life to live in a monastery on the hilltop," then, you can expect some challenges in your life. You can say, "I choose to live in the human world, and I hope that some day my experiences are not so challenging. But, until then, I will do my best to grapple with my challenges with confidence and courage, even if they are very frightening and painful at times. I know that after the challenges are ended— and they *always* end—I will have been benefited in very important ways, even though I may not see the benefit while I am in the middle of the painful challenge." With this attitude, you can actually bring forth a certain amount of joy even when you are grappling with challenges.

❖

Now, it is important to realize that there are some challenges that you may not wish to go forward against. In these, joy is created by *not* engaging the challenge, rather that by engaging the challenge and remembering that you will be benefited by that engagement.

If you are standing in the pathway of an auto in the middle of the street and you say, "This auto should swerve to avoid me," and you do not move, you can curse the auto all you wish, but the auto will still smash you. There are certain "rules" that apply to the human physical world and its challenges, and you ones are wise to abide by them.

If you stand in front of the auto speeding toward you and you say, "I will not move because I am an eternal being and God protects me," you will still be smashed, for God will not manipulate the auto. But, God gives you the intelligence not to stand in front of a speeding auto.

No matter how idealistic you are, no matter how deep your experience of the Divine might be, at times, you can understand that you need to give allegiance to the physical realities of your world. You ones tend to do this naturally. You will not usually stand in front of speeding autos.

But, at times, you do not realize that this same principle applies when you stand in front of "speeding persons"—persons who are strongly unkind, or cruel, or even violent. You have the freedom to choose to try to be idealistic and practice love toward such distorted persons. You can stand in front of them, so to speak, expecting that your love will heal their fear and cause them to "swerve" and not strike out against you. Yet, there is the possibility that you can be "run over" by those who do not care how loving you are. They are so caught in their confusions and fears that all they care about is their own desires, and they can strike out against you, either verbally or physically, no matter how loving you are.

These are temporarily the "laws" of the human world for the deeply confused persons. Even though it is wise for you to keep alive the knowledge that within *every* human being there is an inner core of goodness and the perfection of God Itself, even inside the murderer, you simply would not wish to be the victim of that murderer.

❖

Each day, you ones have such obstacles to your *idealism*. You have the "evidence" that, at least temporarily, the human world can be frightening and threatening, and certainly dangerous to your physical body. However, you must remember that it is never dangerous to your *being*, for your being cannot be diminished or damaged.

But, you may not wish your body to be smashed by an auto, or murdered by a violent person. So, you take steps to protect your body. However, you must be cautious that you do not allow this fear for your physical safety to become a fear of emotional pain that causes you to close your heart to others.

When you have a challenge in which there is no danger to your physical body, then you can be more forceful about moving forward, for the only danger is some emotional pain, and, *emotional pain is temporary*, and, *it cannot damage your being*.

Or, you always have the freedom to choose to step back from even the emotional challenges. You can choose to avoid the emotional pain. That is not bad, and it is not wrong. It is simply smaller, in terms of moving you toward the full power of joy in your life.

Imagine that you have a long-time friend that you love. But, the friend is very critical and often insults you. No matter how much love there is, if you cannot convince the friend to stop attacking you, then you are free to say, "Perhaps I need to step back from this friend and find a new friend." You are not being an unkind or cruel person. You are not betraying the friend. You are not being cowardly in the face of a challenge. You are simply saying, "Given the present realities before me, and the fact that they are not likely to change, I prefer not to be with this friend and suffer unnecessary emotional pain. I will have more joy in my life by avoiding this friend for a while." This example illustrates the freedom that you have in deciding for yourself what to do with various challenges.

❖

You can understand that in human life there are certain *practical realities* that you can approach with the utmost idealism, kindness, and love, and, at times, they cannot be *changed* by you. So, your decision is, "Do I keep trying to work with this unchangeable situation, or, do I change my own pathway in order to have more joy?"

Many sensitive, idealistic, loving persons will usually not give themselves enough leeway to step back from certain areas that are difficult when it might be wise to do so. Most of the time, in most of your situations, and even in relationships of difficulty, it is usually *not* beneficial to step back. You can gain quite a bit from persisting and riding the elephant of challenge to greater growth. But, always in earth life, it is not wise to be overly rigid about any belief, or thought, or idea, no matter how beneficial it is at certain times. At other times, it may not be beneficial.

It is wise to question each moment and each situation, and say, "Here is this wonderful principle of idealism to which I have given allegiance in this lifetime. In this moment and situation, is it best to follow it? Or, is it best to be flexible and consider this to be a unique moment in which I will not do what I normally do. I will do something different for reasons that are important to me." Only *you* can decide what is best here.

You are the one who must decide what is best to do in *every* moment of your life. The important thing is to give yourself permission to address each new situation with the freedom to make new choices and to go in new directions, if you declare that to be best.

Even your strongest ideals, at times, might not be the perfect focus for certain moments. Although, most of the time, it *is* the perfect focus. But, even the highest ideal—which we suggest that you consider to be *love*—might need to be examined closely in certain moments.

Imagine that you meet a stranger in the street, a male one who is poor and hungry. You wish to practice living your ideal of being loving to others, so, you give the one some monies. Then, you invite the one into your home. When he arrives at your home, he beats you and robs you.

If you decide that there is no badness in you being beaten and robbed, you could say, "I will continue to give allegiance to my highest ideal of being loving to others, and I will always make the choices that I made with this male one, and I will not mind being beaten and robbed. I will invite all of the poor ones in the street into my home." That is one way to approach this area of your ideals, but, of course, that approach would be painful for you personally.

A different approach would be to say to yourself, "I am extremely loving, and love is my highest ideal. I believe that love is the answer to all human challenges. I believe that it is the only focus that will bring the beauty of God into human life. But, I will not give everything to this one in the street, because I love *myself*. I love my physical health, I love my money that this one might steal." You could see this, not as a betrayal of your ideal, but as an intelligent way to make a choice about how to live a situation that could be painful and harmful to you personally.

Simply because you are idealistic does not mean that you must turn away from intelligent assessments of the practical situations in your life. You would be wise to integrate a practical experience of the world with your idealism in order to balance your needs against the need of others.

This is quite obvious to most ones, but, occasionally, you might forget it. You might become confused and say, "If I care for my own safety, and wellbeing, and money, I am being selfish. I am betraying my ideal of being loving to everyone." If you do create such confusion, you will need to be flexible with your ideals, and, you will need to be very loving to yourself.

❖

The next area of great importance in drawing upon the power of joy is a deeper understanding of how you *orchestrate* your own human life, consciously or non-consciously.

As you ones may have noticed, you cannot always perfectly manipulate life to fulfill all of your desires. For example, many of you have a desire for more money, yet, you are not achieving it. When you look at such areas where you wish more joy—and you know that you have the power of God Itself within you to orchestrate your own life to achieve that joy— but, at that same time, you clearly see that there are areas where you have tried very hard for many years to make certain fulfillments but you are not making them, then you can begin to wonder if you really *do* have the power to orchestrate your life to please you. You can begin to question, and wonder, "How much power do I really have?"

This is a very delicate and complex area to speak about. So, to begin, we would say: **You *always* have the power to create your own thoughts and feelings, and to decide what actions to take.**

Then, in the face of strong opposing actions by other humans, and in situations over which you have no control, you have the power of *your response*. Usually, you will not be able to force others to perfectly please you, or to change or eliminate situations over which you have no control. But, you always have the power to change your responses to those areas in order to achieve more fulfillment.

Most of you would condemn violence and war in the world. Yet, if you look closely, you will immediately realize that you do not have the power to personally eliminate violence and war. Those are situations over which you have no control. You only have the power to *respond* to those events in ways that help you orchestrate your life in a more satisfying manner.

Imagine that you have a friend who insults you.

You feel deeply wounded. You have such sadness and pain. You could say, "I have the power to communicate with this friend and ask this friend to be kinder." So, you do that, and the friend is kinder to you. All is well. In this case, you have extended your power to orchestrate your life into the choices of another human.

If you communicate gently and lovingly to the friend, asking the one not to insult you, but, the friend says, "I enjoy insulting you and I will not change," then your only power is your *response* to the friend. You could respond by hating and abandoning the friend. You could choose to respond by being more tolerant with the friend, trying not to mind being insulted, and hoping that your love might convince the friend to change. There are many different responses that you could choose.

These dynamics of the day-to-day orchestrating of your life are threads that make up the fabric of your human life. Your life essentially *is* what these threads are. These threads are what your life becomes. How you think, and feel, and choose each day, all of that becomes your life for that day. Even though you are an eternal being, and even though you have extraordinary abilities within you from many lifetimes to create joy, your life in each day will be made up of the thoughts, and feelings, and choices that you make in orchestrating that day. Therefore, no matter how wonderful you are as a *being*, if you constantly create negativity and fear day after day, and you do not live through it and heal it, then you will not orchestrate your life very well, and you can have a miserable life.

❖

The day-to-day practical world is temporarily your arena of expression as a being. It is your playground. So, that is what you need to master in this lifetime.

But, at times, you ones forget how important the simple moments of your life are. In one day, all of those simple moments add up to *that day* of your life, and you need to value that highly. If you made death in that evening, then your last day on earth would have passed by unappreciated.

In some days, you have very large moments, very important experiences. You do notice and appreciate those. But, for most of you, your days are quite simple. You have familiar, repeated actions, and tasks, and interactions with others. For most of you, your days are not extremely dramatic, either positively or negatively. Thus, you can begin to take your life, and yourself, for granted. You can you feel, "There is no importance in what I am doing. I am so ordinary. I am so unimportant." This is where you must be more creative. And, this is where your idealism can be very beneficial.

If you are doing a simple working task in a day, a task that you have done many times before, and you are feeling that it is unimportant, and you cannot manage to stir feelings of appreciation about you or your work, you can gently remind yourself:

"I am doing this task for the reasons that I have in the practical world. But, as I do this, inside me, the great wells and reservoirs of extraordinary experiences from many past lifetimes mingle with this moment that seems so ordinary. *This moment resonates out into eternity.* It is observed and rejoiced in by many souls who love me. The simple action that I am now doing has profound import in so many ways that I can never know. It becomes a part of the fabric of *eternal life.*"

If, in one of your simple moments, you are feeling, "I am not an adequate person," you could imagine that there are many Divine Beings who are sharing your life with you in that moment. *They* are seeing your true magnificence so clearly. *They* know that you are a wonderful and important human *self* walking on earth. Thus, even in a simple moment that seems *negative* to you, you can always remember the goodness that the souls see in you, and you always have the freedom to fill that moment with thoughts and feelings of your larger goodness as an eternal soul temporarily expressing as an important human *self*.

So, often, the creation of more joy in your life is simply a matter of not rushing out to try to do "larger" things in the world, but, to calmly remind yourself that you are an extension of your soul while you are living the simple moments. You are lovingly intertwined with many souls. Inwardly, you are interacting with so many experiences that are important from many past lifetimes that are woven with your experience of the present moment.

There is always layer upon layer, and wave upon wave, of *importance* to even the meanest, most unpleasant moments of your day. Usually, you will not be aware of how important the moment is. You will not be able to feel the significance. But, by simply imagining it, you can create some joy in the moment, and that can inspire you to appreciate you and your life more fully.

So, you might say that your life is a seamless garment in which one thread touches the next, which touches the next, which touches the next—on and on. And, all of it is connected in important ways to the magnificent garment of eternal life.

❖

Questions and Answers

NOTE: Having more joy in life is directly related to how much knowledge a person has about their own mental and emotional patterns. Often, as pointed out in the Guides' answer to the following question, there can be patterns of fear that block a person's knowledge of self. The woman who asked this question had a great deal of experience in the metaphysical area. She wanted more clarity about her psychological makeup.

QUESTION ONE: I have a passion for learning, especially spiritual learning. My favorite subjects are human motivation, people's inner workings, my own potentiality, human spiritual connection, my purpose. It brings me great joy to learn in these areas. I want to ask you to tell me if there are any important things that I don't know about myself, and are there confusions or incorrect beliefs that block my joy that I may need to look at and work with.

THE GUIDES: Imagine that you own a very important book. You have read the first half of that book, but not the last half. You know that you do not *know* the content of the last half, but, *you know where to find that content.*

You have enough intelligence, and enough experience working with your mental and emotional patterns, to know where to find what you do not know. And, usually, you know that the patterns that you are not yet aware of can be hidden behind fears. It is as though you have read the first part of your book and you are in love with the heroine. As you begin to read the second part, you are frightened because the heroine is captured by a villain, so you stop reading and hide the book away.

When you work in this area of uncovering impediments that block fuller joy in your life, patterns that you may not be aware of in your knowledge, begin with uncovering various fears. For, some of those fears have been created *unknowingly* by you in order to avoid certain dark areas of your life that you do not wish to enter into.

For example, you do not wish to know that, at times, you are desperate for love. So, you have tried to be so independent that you can do without love. You pretend that love is not important. You try to act as if you have enough love. There are many different guises that you have put upon this desperation in the love area.

As you work lovingly with your thoughts and feelings, you can gradually become aware of some of your blocking fears and you can release them. For example, you can work with the fear in the love area by telling others that you desire, and *need*, their love. You can *ask* others to love you more deeply. Becoming aware of the fear related to not having enough love, and how you have stiffened emotionally to hide that fear, you can begin to take steps to heal the fear and achieve more love. This illustrates that one of the keys to discovering hidden patterns that block your joy is to look at your various fear patterns.

Now, at this point in your life, since you have brought forth such courage, and strength, and intelligence, and sensitivity, your fears are not dramatically large. We are speaking now of fears about life in the outer world. Your fears of the practical world will fluctuate, of course, depending upon your circumstances. If you lose all of your monies, then fears of poverty will be strong. If you have much money, then there is no fear of poverty. These *outer* areas you need not fret about. You will respond to them when you need to.

The *inner* work that needs to be done is to notice *habits* of fear. So, perhaps once each week, perhaps on a Monday morning, you set aside a "fear discovery" period. You sit in silence and you let your mind freely cast about in any negativity in your life, in the lives of others, in the entire world, and you say to yourself, "I now invite a fear to come into my thoughts and feelings."

Then, simply wait patiently and see what happens. If no fears come forward, then creatively *manufacture* a fear. Say to yourself, "What *could* I be frightened about?" You might decide, "I could be frightened that my mating one makes a sudden death and I am plunged into despair." Create some strong negative thoughts and feelings about that happening and enter the experience of fear. Wallow in it for five moments.

Then, say to yourself, "What I do not know, or what I do not remember about life, in this moment is hidden behind this fear." As you work with this, in this example, you might say, "I do not know that *love is eternal*, or I have forgotten that. So, if this mating one makes sudden death, our love will continue beyond death."

Mostly, these are areas for you to "play" with. We do not see any patterns of unknown confusion, or areas that you are not aware of, that are particularly obstructing of your joy, or that are disruptive in a large sense. Most of the ways that you are learning continue to reveal important truths to you.

So, we would say, mostly celebrate what you *do* know. Mostly celebrate what you are learning. Indulge your passion in these areas. Trust that if there is a significant negative area of unknowing that you need to know about, it will be pointed out by various challenges. So, you need not go out of your way to search it out, or root it out.

❖

NOTE: In the following answer to a woman's question, the Guides show that the degree of joy that each person has is related to discovering their true talents, and to having the confidence to choose which talents to focus on. The Guides describe the woman's talents from past lifetimes, but emphasize that she must decide which ones are important in her present life.

QUESTION TWO: **Would you tell me about the most important themes that my soul has focused upon in my many lifetimes on earth? What are the most important issues and talents for me during this lifetime, and what can I do during this present period to stimulate more feelings of joy?**

THE GUIDES: As we look at this area with you, we could show you certain patterns that *we* believe are extremely important. But, if we do not leave you the freedom to decide for yourself what is important, then, even perfectly following our suggestions would leave you feeling a bit weak, not trusting your own wisdom. So, it is very important that we not interfere with your freedom to declare for yourself what is important in this lifetime.

You must decide what the important *desires* are that you will fulfill, and the talents that you will use to fulfill them. You must decide what accomplishments are important for you to make in this lifetime. So, we must speak in a very general way so as not to interfere with your freedom to choose.

It is as though you would say, "What should I eat for dinner each evening?" If we would specify every meal for you, that would gradually wear away your confidence in making your own choices. So, we can only point to the cupboard and tell you about the different wonderful foods that are in the cupboard. You must decide which ones you will eat.

One of the most interesting focal points that we see—a wonderful food that you have in your cupboard—is your ability *to nurture other human beings*. You often take this talent for granted, or even doubt this ability when you are not feeling deeply loving. Yet, through so many lifetimes on earth, you have been a powerful source of nurturing love and healing for many humans.

At times, you gave this profound goodness in a simple expression as a mother to her children. At other times as a teacher. At other times as a friend. So, one of the strong themes, and, indeed, a strong ability, that you have brought through many lifetimes is the ability to nurture others, to bring them peace, harmony, reassurance, security, stability.

Now, since you, at times, do not even feel the strength of this ability within yourself, you would doubt that you could bring goodness to others in the nurturing area. But, nonetheless, you have been doing that for many years and hardly noticing it.

So, if it pleases you, we suggest that you consider this area of nurturing others to be a very important theme that your soul would hope that you would continue to build upon in this lifetime—a talent that you would continue to appreciate within yourself. The expression of this talent to others has brought you great joy in a number of lifetimes. The blossoming of this talent now will bring you great joy and fulfillment in this lifetime.

The next area, you might call, *a love of beauty*. Through many lifetimes, you have been passionate for beautiful colors, shapes, forms, sounds, people. You have been a one struck by beauty in many lifetimes. This rejoicing in beauty was a source of great joy for you.

In a few lifetimes, you would go a bit "overboard" in your celebration of beauty to the point of being repulsed by ugliness. You would reject ugly persons, ugly things, ugly ideas.

But, in most of the lifetimes, your passion for beauty would thrill you, particularly in periods in which you had the wealth to indulge in beautiful expressions artistically, in terms of the objects in your home—those kinds of areas. These, certainly, were not superficial concerns. For, you could sense often, at times even in this lifetime, that, in a certain way, *beauty is an expression of God that is often **purer** than daily interactions with humans.*

Now, if this is taken too far, of course, it becomes confusing. If you would say, "I love a painting more than a person," you would be confused. But, often, the paintings are *purer* in their beauty than most persons, at least in the persons' negative interactions with others.

You have gravitated toward beauty in many lifetimes because it brought you such joy. And, when you do not have enough beauty in your present life, or you do not see enough beauty in yourself, then there is an unnecessary sadness and feeling of burden, and a great squeezing of your joy. So, if it pleases you, we suggest that you look at beauty as an area to stimulate more joy in your life.

Another strong focus for you is your deep ability to create *companionship*, apart from intimate love. Of course, you might say that the *ideal* companionship for you would be a perfect mating relationship. But, when you are not focused upon that, the "next best" area is perfect friendship. So, you need, perhaps, to look at this area to see if it is one that you can become more passionate about, more confident in, and more fulfilled in, for you have the talent of creating deep companionship that you have brought from past lifetimes.

In many lifetimes, *your passion for knowledge of the Divine* has been the driving force of your life, and you have an ability to gain more knowledge in this area. You have achieved profound experiences of God in a number of lifetimes, and you have helped others awaken to the perfection of God. So, this will be an area that will open the way for more joy as you pay more attention to it.

A certain area that you might tend to underestimate is *physical pleasure*. You have often felt a "sinfulness" about certain sexual expressions. You were "trained" to do that in the past. We are not saying that sensual pleasure is the most important focus in life, but, it is certainly a joyful one for you. You have spent many lifetimes rejoicing in sensual pleasure, not only sexual expression, but, the pleasure of the movement of the body, the warmth of the sun upon the face. These areas are not earthshakingly important, but, added to other areas, they can be very joyful.

Another strong focus for you from the past lifetimes is the area of *children*. Although there has been deep challenge for you in this lifetime in the children area, you need not shy away from it, or be frightened of it. Even small periods of time serving children can be important.

There are many other important talents, and abilities, and themes within you. It is as though you have a tapestry woven of hundreds of different colored threads. If you would say, "Which thread makes the tapestry beautiful?" we would say that it is *every one of them*.

You have so many different threads to choose from in weaving your present tapestry of life on earth. *You* must decide which ones are the most important, the most beautiful, and which ones you wish to give the most attention to in this lifetime.

❖

The Guides' Closing Teaching

In considering the many patterns within your human *self* that will affect how much you draw upon the power of joy, you could say that it is similar to certain waves from the sea breaking upon the shore. First, there is a small wave, then next, a one that is a bit larger. After that, a larger one, and then another larger one, on and on, until there is a giant wave.

This symbolizes what you ones might call the "experiential momentum" of your human life. And, that momentum applies to many different aspects of the daily lives of your ones. Some of you have great momentum in the personal love area, while others have small momentum in the love area. Some have great momentum in their occupation, some small. Some have great momentum in artistic expression, some small. Some have great momentum in awakening to the soul, some small.

At times, you ones can be *very strong* in any area. That is the giant wave. At other times, the giant wave passes and smaller ones begin the process of building toward another giant wave. That is the ever-shifting inner momentum of your daily life in the world.

If you work patiently with yourself, opening to your true magnificence, healing any patterns of fear, then, on the average, you will have a rather large momentum in the *important* areas of your life. You might feel weak, or depleted, in some other areas, but, generally, you will use your inner wisdom to keep bringing your abilities forward in the areas of your

life that are most important to you and to your soul.
And, as you attain more and more mastery in the
important areas, then you will be infusing the power
of joy into your experience day by day.

❖

For this moment, it is important to bring forth a
feeling of joy into your sense of being *you* in this
lifetime. To do that more satisfactorily, no matter
how you might feel about not being good enough in
some areas, you need to feel now that you are doing
very well overall in living your life.

For some of you, this might mean that you *ignore*
certain old thoughts that you have created about *who
you are*. These would be thoughts that would say, "I
am not a good person. I do not have a purpose in my
life. I will never succeed in life." Although you can
mistakenly believe that you are accurately describing
who you are, *those thoughts are not truths*. They are
distorted and confused negative thoughts that you
have created about yourself because you have not seen
your true *goodness* as a human *self*.

Then, there are negative thoughts that you can
create about *what you are doing* in your life. If you
would say, "I am not earning enough money to please
me," then, that might be a *fact*. But, if you mingle
that with distorted thoughts about who you are and
you say, "I am an inadequate person because I am not
earning enough money," then that is *not* a fact. That
is a confused and distorted perception of *who you are*,
related to a negative perception of *what you are doing*.

You must be very clear in these areas. If there are *factual* aspects of your life that do not please you, as when you would say, "I am sad because I am failing to achieve wealth," then you can work with that factual area and try to achieve more wealth. But, be very alert for any thoughts or feelings that you create in *response* to those facts that would say, "Because I am not achieving wealth, I am failing as a human, I am not a good person, I am inadequate, I am unworthy." *Those are never true.* They are always distorted perceptions of who you truly are as a human *self*.

Whenever you notice such self-diminishments, pounce upon them. Be honest with them. Take five moments to fully experience the negative thoughts and feelings about yourself that you have created. For five moments, feel miserable about yourself. Condemn yourself. Curse yourself if you wish. Imagine that you are the worst person on the face of this earth. Wallow in those negative thoughts and feelings for five moments.

Then, calm yourself and say, "These are my distorted thoughts and feelings, not truths. No thought or feeling in this life can diminish the magnificence of my being. No thought or feeling can restrict the love of God Itself that pours into me. But, many thoughts and feelings can temporarily *distract* me from that love and cause me to believe that it does not exist."

❖

You must be very careful in working with self-diminishment patterns. You do not wish to delude yourself by pretending that you have no negative thoughts and feelings at all about yourself. But, on the other hand, you do not wish to be a slave to self-created negative thoughts and feelings about you.

Each day, you need a bit of time to occupy with self-created negative thoughts and feelings about you, depending upon how persistent they are. The degree of persistence will determine how much time you need, and, *you* will decide that.

Most of the time, when you are *not* criticizing yourself, you need to be *celebrating* yourself. You need to be as eager to find a reason for celebrating yourself as you usually are to find a reason for criticizing yourself. You must take note of how much actual time you spend during the day in self-diminishment, and, you must insist that you spend at least equal time—and hopefully more than that—in *self-appreciation, self-enlivenment.*

You have the power to *create* the self-appreciating thoughts and feelings. You do not need to sit and wait for your soul, or God, to plant them into you. You can either use your inner power to criticize yourself, or you will use it to appreciate your goodness.

❖

At the end of each day, you need to observe that day and ask yourself, "How much time did I spend in self-diminishment in this day? How much time did I spend in self-appreciation?" If you see that the time spent in self-diminishment is larger, then you need to make some changes. You owe this to yourself. If you do not give the self-appreciation to yourself, then you are cheating yourself, and, you are diminishing the joy that you will experience in this lifetime.

There are many ways to achieve joy in human life, and there are many human ways to block the joy. The quickest way to block joy is self-diminishment, self-condemnation. The quickest way to expand joy is self-appreciation, self-enlivenment.

In appreciating yourself, you do not need to pretend that you appreciate your negative *actions* in the world. You can take a few moments to condemn those, if you wish. Then, say to yourself:

> "*I am not my actions.* I am a Divine being who is temporarily taking human actions that do not please me. I will change those actions. They are temporary. But, I am *always* a Divine being. I am always an extension of the Forces of God, temporarily expressing in human form. Nothing can change that."

In this moment, you can begin the greatest joy that a human can have by feeling that *you are the perfection of God Itself,* and that will never change. You can ignore it, disbelieve it, turn away from it. But, it will never change.

So, in this moment, we suggest that you believe in it, and turn toward it. Use your imagination to envision your great inner goodness. And, as we embrace you now, as we pour our love into your heart, imagine *the true goodness and perfection of you.* Imagine the goodness of God Itself at the core of your human *self.* Know that it radiates out in all directions, in all realms, in all worlds.

Imagine that now as we love you and guide you. And, know that this is the center of your joy, and you can return to it whenever you please, day by day, throughout this lifetime.

And, for this time in earth, the speaking is ended.

❖ ❖ ❖

CHAPTER 10

The Tenth Reading

NOTE: There were no questions asked during this final Reading of the Retreat.

The Guides' Final Teaching

As you consolidate your experiences of this period of focusing upon the healing power of joy, it is natural to do so in the familiar manners that you have learned in this lifetime. All ones, in their daily lives, will bring their old patterns into new experiences.

So, if you are a one who consistently *doubts*, and you have had some new inspirational experiences from this period together, then, later, you might begin to doubt those experiences. If you are a one who usually lets experiences of truth touch you and inspire you, then you will take the experiences from this grouping and you will build greater truth upon them. If you are a one who consistently opens to love, then you will take these experiences, allow them to penetrate you deeply, and expand the feelings of love.

Each human, in their own way, will "internalize"

255

the new experiences that they have in life, and there will be "ripples" of old thoughts and feelings that mingle with the new experiences.

To expand your experience of joy in your life, you can ask yourself to respond to inspirational experiences in a new way. You can engage those experiences in a fresh manner, not allowing old limited thoughts and feelings to color them. That is how you can invite a *newness* into your life that can expand all areas of your experience.

For example, if you have some deep inspirational experiences, but then you say, "Since I am a doubting one, perhaps I need to consider that these experiences are not real, perhaps they will fade away and I will simply be an ordinary, limited person," you can give a few moments to doubting the experiences. But, then, say to yourself, "What are some *new* ways that I can respond to these inspirational experiences, to think about them and feel about them without my old pattern of doubting?"

Remembering the inner reservoir of power and potency that we have pointed out that lives within you, you might say, "I could create *any* new response that pleases me. I could even have a new response that would say that the inspiring experiences that I have had are rooted in the truth of God. The deep openings that I have made will be permanent. I will take them forth into my day-to-day life in a way that will cause a seeding of ever-new inspirational experiences."

You are free to create this powerful new response. Of course, if you insist upon allowing old limited patterns to dominate you, then you are free to say, "I rejoice in these inspirational experiences, but I expect them to be short-lived. When I return to my daily life, I expect to fall back into my unsatisfying ways of living." That kind of attitude will send you back into limited experiences.

It is not that you ones must fuss and fret about how you respond to inspirational experiences. You simply need to remember that if you are not pleased with your responses, then you have the power to make some changes, to think in new ways, and feel in new ways. This can help you feel very joyful about your capacity to continue to build upon important awakenings, openings, insights, that you have achieved by your willingness to engage in inspirational experiences.

❖

There are four focal points that we will show you that, regardless of your personal choice about how to respond to your inspirational experiences, will help you go forward with more joy, from this point on, for the remainder of your life. Some of you tend toward these areas. These are ways to crystallize your thinking about them.

The **first focal point** is: *Paying more loving attention to yourself.* Do not do that to search out flaws in yourself to eliminate. If you have some areas that do not please you and you wish to change them,

then change them. But, you can make a promise to
yourself that says:

> "I will pay more attention to the *inner goodness*
> of myself as a being. I will look for that goodness
> each day, and I will expect to find it more and
> more. I will make plans each day that allow me
> the opportunity to spend a few moments seeing
> my magnificence, instead of being distracted by
> the complexities of my life."

This focal point will free you to say to yourself:

> "I owe it to myself as a child of God to enjoy the
> magnificence of God that lives within me while
> I am temporarily alive in this human form. If I
> do not notice this Divine gift, then I will be
> squeezing the joy out of my life."

This is as though you go to a grand ball and
there is one special person that you wish to dance
with. But, throughout the evening, you become
distracted dancing with many others. Then, the
dance is over. Now, it is not wrong, or bad, that you
did not dance with the special person. But, it is
smaller than what you hoped to experience at the
ball. Had you paid more attention to what you were
doing, then you would certainly have had the joy of
dancing with that special one.

In this life, you ones have many interests, many
focal points, many dancing partners at the ball of life.
And, that is wonderful. But, if you forget the *special*
experience—the great joy of experiencing *the
perfection of God Itself living inside your human self*—

then you will cheat yourself. You will have a smaller dance of human experience in this lifetime.

You will have many important things that you occupy with in your day-to-day life. But, what could be more important and more joyful than feeling the majesty of *all that is*, the *perfect Divine Love*, the *ongoing beauty and harmony of the Forces of God Itself* filling you? What in daily life could be more important, more fulfilling than that?

So, the first focus to wielding the power of joy in your life is simply to give some loving attention to yourself so that you can awaken to your true inner goodness that streams into your human *self* from the forces of your soul, and from God Itself.

❖

The **second focal point** is: *Dispelling the illusion of separation* by a patient, diligent deepening of love with other humans.

Most of you do give some attention to this. But, at times, you forget how important it is to have loving experiences with others. You become so occupied in other areas of your life. Certainly, that is not an error. But, you would not wish to go too long, too many days, without giving loving attention to the humans about you. You need to savor the opportunity to feel a wonderful loving connectedness with other humans.

Now, at times, *you must take the initiative* to bring about this important experience. As you may have noticed, there are a number of humans about you in your daily life who have not made it a priority in their lives to have a loving interaction with you. Many of them have the priority of seeking their own fulfillments quite aggressively. Or, they have the priority of brooding upon their own inner life, or many other areas that distract them from paying attention to you.

If you make a commitment to this second focal point, you can become the one who *initiates* softer, more sensitive communications with other humans. If you remember how important this is, and you remember that the human years pass swiftly and then you leave this lifetime, that will spark you to make the loving relationships an important focus in each day.

In a sense, each human is rushing toward physical death. When you go a day without savoring the humans that you come in contact with, without trying to reach out to them with a gentle, inviting, loving communication, then you cheat yourself of a wonderful opportunity to feel that you are surrounded by loving brothers and sisters. Not only is reaching out in this manner the way to stimulate more joy for you, but, it reminds others that they are not alone. It makes them more interested in opening and sharing their hearts.

Each day, you might make a small plan for how you can reach out to others in a loving way. For example, if you have a consistent working arena where you encounter the same persons day after day, then, before you enter that working arena, you can make a plan that would say, "Today, I will encounter the following persons," and you list them by name in your mind: Mary, John, Bill, Sue, and so forth. You realize that they are all quite familiar to you, and you might even tend to take them for granted. But, as you make your plan, you ask yourself, "What would be a way that I could show more warmth individually to each of these ones, a way *that would be comfortable for them?*"

Let us say that there is a female one who is your supervisor. She is a bit formal and retiring. She is not demonstrative. In making your plan, you are free to say, "It would be wonderful for me to rush toward her, lift her in an embrace, and say 'I love you madly.'" That might be interesting for you, but it would not be so wonderful for her. You must always adjust your reaching out to others with a great sensitivity to the individual and their patterns.

In this example, as you make your plan, you might decide, "It would be acceptable to her simply to place my hand on her arm and say, today I believe you appear very attractive. Your hair is very attractive. This is a small expression that might be appreciated."

If there is a one in your working arena with whom you are friends, and you ones often embrace, in that day you might say, "You make a very loving experience for me in my day, and I appreciate sharing my life with you in this working arena."

As you practice the loving expression to others,

you become a bringer of *Spiritual Light*. You are actually reminding many who have forgotten, that you are their brother or sister, that you are a wonderful part of their life.

❖

The **third focal point** for expanding the joy in your life is: *Creating an ongoing dialogue with your soul.* Some of you now do this in various ways, but you might wish to flesh it out a bit more with your imagination.

In alignment with your personal needs and beliefs, you might wish to imagine that your soul is a most extraordinary father with great power and authority, and, with a perfect love for you. Or, depending upon your needs, you might imagine your soul as the most perfect nurturing mother, and a mother who loves you constantly. You can use whatever imaginings about your soul that touch you.

After creating the vision of your soul that touches you, then you would speak to your soul often throughout your day. Usually, you would not speak out loud if you are in public.

For example, as you awaken in a morning, you could say, "My dear soul, I so thank you for giving me this opportunity to live in this physical body. I thank you for sharing my human experience with me as I go forward into this day."

The dialog that you create with your soul will often be influenced by your needs of the moment. For example, if you have been rejected by a loved one and you are feeling great despair, you might say, "Dear soul, please pour forth your love more strongly into me now, for I am feeling so sad and alone. I need to know that you love me, so I ask you to intensify the energy of love that you are pouring into me."

These are gentle, simple suggestions for fleshing out the experience of communion with your soul by using thoughts, and words, and images. You can do this in a relaxed, trusting manner throughout your day. And, you can do it light-heartedly, of course.

❖

The **fourth focal point** is difficult to put into human words, for each of you has your own unique ways of thinking in this human world. So, we would say that the need here is to "*turn yourself inside out.*"

Imagine that you are looking at your human *self* from outside of you. You are seeing your *self* as *a large sphere of light*. On the *surface* of that sphere are your conscious thoughts, feelings, experiences that you share with other humans. They are all rooted in your experience in the *physical* world. Throughout your life, most of your daily experiences are on that surface of the sphere of light as you move about in earth.

Then, beneath that surface "layer" of the sphere would be another layer that would be your private thoughts and feelings that are *not* shared with other humans. This is the layer that you could think of as your private personal life.

Beneath that, there would be a layer that you

could imagine as what many humans consider to be the "subconscious." In this layer, there are those things in you that you do not consciously know in the moment, but you believe that they are there. These things could be forgotten experiences from the outer surface layer. They could be forgotten experiences from the private personal layer.

Then, beneath that subconscious layer—moving inward in this sphere of light that represents your human *self*—is a layer of what you might call your "hidden inner resources." This would be your many talents and abilities placed into your human *self* by your soul. In this layer, there would be your memories of past lifetimes on earth. Usually, the "contents" of this layer are very difficult to become consciously aware of. So, you will need to *imagine* then.

At times, you ones do bring some of your talents and abilities forth from this deeper layer of the sphere of light toward the surface. They become conscious to you, and you realize that you have a talent for a certain kind of human expression. Then, you can bring that talent forward as actions that you take on the surface layer of conscious experience in the physical world. So, with certain of the talents from this deeper layer, a layer that usually remains unknown to you, you can bring them all the way through the various layers to the outer surface and actually live them out in your daily life.

Occasionally, some of you can bring forth some

memories from past lifetimes from this inner layer of the sphere. You can become consciously aware of experiences that you have had in past lifetimes on earth.

In this layer of the sphere of your human *self*, you would also have what you might call "guiding impulses" from your soul. *You-as-a-soul* have chosen certain impulses for your present human *self* to nudge you toward the more important fulfillments of life. For example, here might live a non-conscious impulse to help others heal their pain. During your life, you might bring that impulse up through the various levels until it becomes a conscious desire in the layer of your private personal life. Then, you could choose to act upon that desire in the outer layer of experience in the physical world.

❖

We are attempting to describe a certain kind of *process* for you. You can think of it as a process of "movement" through the imagined layers in the sphere of light that represents various aspects of your human *self*.

To go further in your imagining, you can imagine that the *outer* layer of the sphere of light, the layer that represents your surface life in the physical world, has the *dimmest* light.

Beneath that, you could imagine that the layer that represents your private inner life has a light that is a bit brighter than the outer layer.

Then, the next layer beneath that, which represents your "subconscious"—the layer where there are the forgotten experiences from the outer layers that are not immediately available to your conscious awareness—you could imagine as being brighter in light than the outer layers.

The layer beneath that, where you would have your hidden talents, memories from past lifetimes, and the guiding impulses from your soul, you could envision as being even brighter in light that the outer layers.

Then, you could envision, at the very center, the core, of the whole sphere of light that represents your human *self*, the most bright, brilliant, beautiful, true, and perfect light. This core of perfect light would represent your true *being* as a human *self*. It is the pure *soul-energy-structure* that enables you to feel, "I am *me*."

Certain aspects of your true *self* that, at times, come up from this center of pure, brilliant perfection into the outer layer of your conscious awareness, enable you to feel that what is *you* has a certain magnificent sense of goodness in it. However, your conscious experience of those wonderful inner qualities at the core of your human *self* can fluctuate because they have been "filtered" through many layers on their way to your conscious awareness.

If you had *no* confused layers of human consciousness and personal complexity, then you would *constantly* experience the central core of perfection within you. You would say without any doubt, "I am a *perfect* being. I have no flaws or failings." If you experienced *only* the core of your human *self*, you would have no illusions, and, there would be no barriers to your perception of the Divine Realm. You would be similar to your soul, but encased in a human *self* in which you would say, "I am *me*, and I am *one* perfect being, and I am not the rest of the human beings on this earth."

In other words, your inner core of your human *self* holds a perfect experience, but, it is a perfect experience that is temporarily experienced as *apart* from the full unity of all of life. This enables you to have the experience of being a unique individual. It enables you to have what you could call an "ego," in the *positive* sense.

This inner core of purity within you is *a direct infusion* of Divine energies from your soul. It is uncluttered, unconfused, untainted. However, this inner core of perfection must "seep up" through the other layers of your human *self* sphere in order to eventually become an aspect of your *conscious* life on the surface of the sphere. Thus, your conscious experience of that inner perfection of you can have various temporary confusions and distortions that accumulate as those Divine energies "pass through" certain non-conscious energies of negativity from past lifetimes of earth, and through confusions in your private inner life, and through challenges in the surface world—all of that.

By imagining this sphere of light with its many

different layers, with its "beginning" to your conscious awareness appearing on the outer surface where it is dimmer and where you put most of your attention each day, and moving inward through the various layers to the inner core where it is perfectly pure and bright but where you usually put no attention, you can see what we mean by "turning yourself inside out." By awakening to the true goodness of you in the center core, and bringing *that* into the outer layer of your conscious awareness where you put attention upon it, your experience of life is opened to the full power of joy that is available to you.

❖

It would be wise for you ones, perhaps two or three times each day, to make a gentle silence for a moment or two in which you say to yourself, "In this moment, I do not wish to occupy with the outer layers of my sphere of light that are dimmer and less perfect. I wish to turn myself inside out and bring the inner core of perfection to the surface level of my conscious awareness."

This is another way to use words to try to help you *feel* the truth of the Divine energies of which you are made. This turning inside out can be very joyful. Then, when you add it to the other areas that you have learned about your true goodness, you can have a very strong acceleration of joy in your day-to-day life. However, in daily life in the complexities of the physical world, you can always expect *fluctuations* in your experience of joy.

Imagine that you are a one who rides the waves of the sea on a board. As you float in the water, there comes a very large wave and you place your board upon it. Then, you have the most joyful, exciting ride. However, you do not expect that single wave to continue for hours. You know that the wave will break, and then you will come down from the height of the wave and you will experience less joy. Then, you search out another large wave to ride.

So, even as you ones, in your inspired moments, go forth to make a large wave of joy in the coming period, you need not be surprised when the wave breaks and you feel that you are losing some of the momentum of your inspiration. Usually, this is caused by temporarily forgetting to use the focal points on the power of joy that help you ride the wave in an inspiring way.

When the sense of less joy does come forth in your experience, you would need to say, "I expected this downturn as a natural rhythm, and I will ride the trough with as much intensity as I rode the crest of the wave." Even during a less joyful period, you can continue to make your learning, your growing, your adjusting, your healing. Then, eventually, you will remember the ways to release the limits, to free yourself from the heaviness that you have accumulated. And, you will find another wave of joy and you will ride that.

❖

Experiencing fluctuations in joy is the nature of human life in the physical world. So, when you have the peaks and valleys, you need not say, "There must be something wrong with me for I am not able to continually maintain higher levels of joy. I always seem to fall back to feelings of heaviness, or confusion, or frustration." With some deeper thinking, you would be able to understand that there is nothing wrong with you at all. You are simply human, and it is human to ride the waves of mental-emotional shifting and changing. But, with what you are learning about the power of joy, you should be able to make the trough of the wave less deep and the crest of the wave higher.

Each day, *take responsibility for your own joy*. You can ask others to help you be joyful. You can often ride upon their waves at times. But, say to yourself quite often:

> **"I have the power of God Itself within my ability to think, and feel, and choose. It pleases me to choose *more joy* for myself in each day, and I intend to do that with a patient, determined commitment to myself."**

❖

In this moment of time, we are celebrating the many areas of awakening that you ones are stirring within yourselfs. We are celebrating the courage that you have shown to peel back some layers of emotional protection to feel the love of brothers and sisters together. We are celebrating your sincerity, your hunger for truth and perfection.

We now ask that you make a wonderful feeling that you are joining us in celebrating *you*. You are feeling more clearly how truly wonderful you are as a human being. You are seeing, and appreciating, how you try so hard to create goodness in this world each day that you live in it.

We ask now that you try to become aware of the wonderful inner glow, the beautiful, pure, shining inner portion of your extraordinary human *self* that is so beautiful. You can know that this magnificence is *always* there within you, beneath whatever layers that you are living through in the moment. And, remember that this beautiful inner core of you *is where you meet your soul*. *You-as-a-soul* share this inner core of Divine energy with your human *self*. *You-as-a-soul* sustain that inner core. So, as you are willing to turn yourself inside out and enter that beautiful, perfect, brilliant light of love at the core of your human *self*, you are actually merging with a portion of your Divine soul.

In this moment, we ask that you imagine and feel that you are doing that, as we are now loving you and guiding you. Feel that you are peeling away all outer layers. The perfect goodness and love of your true being is coming to the surface of your awareness. You can now feel it within your body, within your heart. You can feel the goodness, beauty, and love of your soul within you.

As you do that in this moment, affirm within

your own consciousness that you can do that in *any* moment, day by day, throughout your present human lifetime.

As we love you now, release. Give yourself to the perfection within you, and feel the Divine Love of your soul, of many souls, and of God Itself, as it fills you and lifts you in this moment of time.

And, for this time in earth, the speaking is ended

❖ ❖ ❖

www.ingramcontent.com/pod-product-compliance
Lightning Source LLC
Chambersburg PA
CBHW051415090426
42737CB00014B/2674